OUTLINES

OF

PSYCHOLOGY

OUTLINES

OF

PSYCHOLOGY

DICTATED PORTIONS

OF THE

LECTURES OF HERMANN LOTZE

TRANSLATOR

GEORGE T. LADD

GYAN

Published by

GYAN

Gyan Publishing House
5, Ansari Road
Daryaganj, New Delhi-110002
Phone: 011-47034999, 9811692060
E-mail: books@gyanbooks.com

Distribution Network
gyanbooks.com
India, USA, Canada, UK, Australia

ISBN: 978-93-7097-463-0 (PB)

First Published, 1886

2nd Impression 2025

Printed at: Gyan Press, Delhi.

OUTLINES OF PSYCHOLOGY

TRANSLATOR-GEORGE T. LADD

LOTZE'S

OUTLINES OF PHILOSOPHY

IV

PSYCHOLOGY

OUTLINES

OF

PSYCHOLOGY

DICTATED PORTIONS

OF THE

LECTURES OF HERMANN LOTZE

TRANSLATED AND EDITED BY

GEORGE T. LADD

PROFESSOR OF PHILOSOPHY IN YALE COLLEGE

BOSTON
GINN & COMPANY
1886

EDITOR'S PREFACE.

THE "Outlines of Psychology" was the first to appear of that series of eight small volumes of *Dictate* from the lectures of Lotze, which followed each other in rapid succession after their author's death. The present translation is from the German of the third edition, published at Leipzig, by S. Hirzel, in 1884. The first German edition was issued in the early Fall of 1881. It consisted mainly of the lecture-notes of Robert Lotze, a son of the philosopher, who attended his father's course in Psychology for the Winter Semester of 1880–81, and who testifies in the Preface that he recorded them as they were formulated by the lecturer himself. The volume was, however, before publication, subjected to the thorough revision of Professor Rehnisch, Lotze's colleague in Göttingen. The third German edition of the "Outlines of Psychology" is somewhat changed, in certain passages, from the first; in particular, some difficult points — for example, the rise and nature of our mental picture of ourselves, in Chap. vi., "The Feelings" — have been more fully explained. All three editions, however, are throughout substantially, and for the most part even verbally, the same.

It is not likely that any other compend of truths touching the science of Mind, at once so brief and so comprehensive, is to be found in all the literature of the subject. I am sure that there is no other by so mature and competent an authority. By preference, native facility, training, and practice, Lotze was almost incomparably well fitted to deal with the great science of Psychology. In his biographical and eulogistic sketch of Lotze (contained in the appendix to the "Outlines of Æsthetics"), Professor Rehnisch speaks of this as the "darling lecture-course" of its lamented author. First and last, directly and indirectly, far more of Lotze's published work deals with the human soul as its subject than with any other philosophical inquiry. He may fitly be called a born psychologist. He had the delicate tact, the reflective insight, the subtlety in analysis of mental states, which psychology demands for its successful cultivation. Moreover, his training was of that comprehensive kind which alone makes it possible to look upon the many-sided human mind from all of its many sides. Like more than one other notable philosopher (and among them all by far most notable — Aristotle), Lotze was the son of a physician. He was thoroughly versed in the sciences of human physiology and human pathology. His early lecture-courses included these subjects. While a young man at Leipzig, we find him offering instruction in "pastoral medicine," therapeutics, general pathology, "juridical medicine," and the functions and diseases of the nervous system. His published works include treatises on the Philosophical Principles of Biology, on Life and Vital Force, on General Physiology and Medical Psychology, and on Life and Mechanism, etc. He was thoroughly acquainted with all that modern science has done for the study of mind by opening the approaches to it from the experimental and physiological points of view.

But Lotze was equally well equipped by nature and cultivation to discuss the metaphysical problems which enter into the study of psychology and which so largely impart to it its peculiar value and charm. While admitting the help of objective experimental methods, he did not depreciate the instrument of self-consciousness. While proposing a brilliant exposition of nature's method of giving to us our ideas of the spatial qualities and relations of objects, in his theory of so-called "local signs," he detected the fallacies of all attempts — whether *a priori* or *a posteriori* — at the so-called "deduction of space." The offences against metaphysic which are committed by all materialistic views when introduced into psychology were patent to Lotze.

The third Part of his large work on Metaphysic, and considerable portions of his Logic and of the Microcosmus, are treatises on psychology. I doubt whether any one workman of the century is entitled to higher esteem than Lotze for the quantity and quality of his teaching regarding the nature of Mind.

The attention of the reader is called to the wide range of the subjects touched upon within the limits of this brief treatise. The second or theoretical part of the "Outlines of Psychology" includes chapters on the Seat of the Soul, its reciprocal Relations to the Body, its Essential Nature, and even on the Realm of Souls. Accustomed as we are to see almost all the available space in psychological treatises appropriated to the details of the phenomena of intellect, it may appear strange that any space can be given in so brief a compend to subjects such as these. We shall do well to remember, however, that *these* are just the subjects into which we all desire to look. It is the teacher's business then to try to hold open — at least wide enough for a glimpse — through the door between the soul's self-conscious activity and the soul's real self.

No other one of Lotze's philosophical Outlines is

more nearly complete and symmetrical than this. But it is, of course, only a brief presentation of *outlines*. It will be a pleasure and a reward to the translator, if the perusal of this small work shall result in an increased study of the more voluminous psychological writings of its distinguished author.

TABLE OF CONTENTS.

INTRODUCTION.

§ 1. Sensations, ideas, feelings, and acts of will, constitute the well-known facts, the whole of which we are accustomed to designate, although with the proviso of future proof, as the life of a peculiar entity, called 'the Soul.'

The requirements of science would be perfectly satisfied, —

(1) in case we could, as exact observation directs us, furnish a complete exhibition of all the single elements of this life and of the general forms in which they are combined (*Descriptive* or *Empirical* Psychology); —

(2) in case we could tell the nature of the subject of this entire life, as well as the efficient forces and conditions by which it is produced and compelled to keep within those forms of its course that are known empirically (*Explanatory, Mechanical* or *Metaphysical* Psychology) · and, finally, —

(3) in case we could specify what is the rational meaning for which all this exists, or the vocation which the life of the soul in general has to fulfil

in the totality of the world (*Ideal* or *Speculative* Psychology).

Since the last of the foregoing problems does not admit of a solution in strictly scientific form, and the treatment of the first may conveniently be combined with that of the second, the essential question with which we are to be occupied is the following: Under what conditions, and by means of what forces, do the individual processes of the spiritual life originate; and how do they combine with and modify each other, and by such coöperation bring to pass the whole of the spiritual life?

We choose our way, however, so as to follow the course of the thing itself; that is to say, we speak first of the external impressions by which the spiritual activity is at every moment aroused anew, then of the manifold internal elaboration which these impressions undergo, finally of the reflex activities, motions, and other actions, which result from them. It is only after passing in review these single elements of the spiritual life that it is possible to give a comprehensive exposition of the interior nature of the subject which leads this life.

PART FIRST.

THE SINGLE ELEMENTS OF THE INNER LIFE.

Part First.

THE SINGLE ELEMENTS OF THE INNER LIFE.

CHAPTER I.

OF SIMPLE SENSATIONS.

§ 2. By 'simple sensations' we understand, in this place, those in whose content no composite structure out of parts, whether dissimilar or similar, is to be observed: and we further conceive of such sensations — for so the case customarily is — as induced by external impressions.

In such a case we distinguish, as the primary process in the originating of sensations, the external sense-stimulus. Nothing becomes an object of perception by means of its bare existence: everything becomes such only by being either itself brought near to the point of contact with our body, as is the case of impact; or else by imparting to a medium, which surrounds it, certain motions that are transplanted from element to element in this medium, and that finally reach our body, — as is the case with waves of sound and light. In all cases, however, such external sense-stimulus consists in some form or other of the motion of certain masses of matter: and it possesses in itself no similarity to the spiritual processes that are to result from it.

§ 3. The second process which is necessary is that within the body which the external stimulus excites.

On its entrance into the superficial parts of our body, the external stimulus produces manifold changes in the most external layers of its covering, — changes of which we know little, and which we do not need to investigate from the psychological point of view. For none of them become the occasions of sensations until they reach the ends of the nerve-fibres that are distributed everywhere throughout the body, and produce in these fibres an excitation which must be propagated along the entire course of the nerve-thread up to the brain, if a sensation is to originate. Every injury to the nerve which prevents such propagation of the impulse has, therefore, also the effect of rendering all stimulation of the peripheral nerve-ending completely inoperative so far as consciousness is concerned. Now we do not know with definiteness in what the aforesaid excitation, the so-called 'nerve-process,' consists; and it is of importance for psychology merely to inquire, whether this process is simply a process of physical motion, or whether it from the beginning participates in the character of the spiritual life.

Now a sensation cannot exist in the nerve in a merely general form, but it must be accurately specified precisely *who* is to *have* the sensation. The nerve as a whole cannot be this subject; because the nerve is an aggregate of many parts, and besides, it is by no means all at one time in the condition of excitation. On the contrary, one part after the other is affected in succession. Nothing more, therefore, could possibly be asserted than that each indivisible atom of the nerve is a 'sensitive subject,' and imparts its own sensation to its neighbor until finally it arrives at the soul.

Since, however, this propagation of the excitation can be prevented by altering the physical continuity of the nerve—for example, by section of it—it is also undoubtedly not the result of an immediate sympathy, but of a physical influence which one nerve-atom **a** exercises upon the next atom **b**, etc. We should accordingly be compelled to say: The atom **a** acts physically upon **b**; in consequence of its suffering this influence, **b** is thrown into a state of sensation **S**; and, again, in consequence of that, **b** exerts a new physical impact upon **c**, which in turn is by this means induced to the sensation **S** and in consequence thereof to the exercise of a physical impact upon the atom **d**. The last nerve-atom **z** would then act, in a manner as yet quite obscure, upon the soul, and stir this, too, to produce *its* sensation **S**.

Now it is obvious that this last impact by means of which *our* sensation (the only one of which we actually know anything) originates in us, will have had its result quite as truly if the nerve-atoms should exercise merely a physical influence upon each other, and if sensations of their own (which are merely empty conjectures and not demonstrated facts) should be wholly dispensed with.

Since, therefore, these sensations peculiar to the nerves contribute nothing whatever to the explanation of *our own* sensation, and besides are not demonstrable, while the propagation of a physical impact cannot be denied; we shall in future consider the nerve-process also as merely a process of physical motion, that is carried over from one particle of the nerve to another, and as yet has nothing of the psychical character which belongs to the sensation that follows it.

§ 4. The third member of this chain of processes is, now, the state of consciousness so well known to us all, the sensation itself, — the 'seeing' of a light of definite color or the 'hearing' of a sound.

Of the two elements in the latter process which we can distinguish in our thinking, — namely, the qualitative content of which we have an experience in sensation and the activity in sensation by means of which we are conscious of this content, — neither the one nor the other is comparable with the nature of the external stimulus or of the neural process. However accurately, too, we may analyze the nature of the waves of ether, we never discover in it a reason why it must be seen as brightness and not rather heard as sound; and just as little, why some waves must be experienced as the sensation red, and others as the sensation blue,—and not the reverse. Further: however we may combine physical motions of nerve-atoms with one another, there never comes a point at which it would be comprehensible as a matter of course, that the motion last produced is bound to remain *motion* no longer, and must rather pass over into this process of sensation so totally different in kind.

All efforts to demonstrate how it comes about that the merely physical motion gradually passes over into sensation are, therefore, wholly in vain. We must rather be satisfied with asserting that a necessity of nature, which has hitherto wholly escaped our knowledge, has in fact united these two series of processes, — the motions and the sensations, — incomparable and irreducible to each other as the two are; and has done this in such a way that a definite member of the one series always has for its consequent a definite member of the other.

§ 5. It is now, however, to be assumed that these two series of processes will not be concatenated wholly without some controlling principle; that rather similar sensations will correspond to similar stimuli, and different sensations to different stimuli; and that in cases where a definite increase, interference, periodicity, or prominent point exists in the series of stimuli, all these will find expression in some way or other in the series of sensations also.

Empirically we are able as yet to establish the foregoing conjecture to only a very limited extent.

In the first place, the various classes of sensations (colors, tones, smells) exist without intervening terms and as a bare matter of fact, side by side with each other; and they do not constitute a closed system. For example, from the fact that we experience waves of ether as light, it does not in the least degree follow that we must consequently experience waves of air as sound.

The same thing is true of the single members of the particular classes. He who had merely had the sensation of 'sour' or of 'yellow,' would not thereby be led to the thought that there must be also 'bitter' and 'blue.'

Further, that a definite increase in the sensations corresponds to a definite increase in the series of stimuli we observe to be true only in the case of tones, the pitch of which rises with the number of the vibrations of the acoustic waves. On this matter it deserves to be remarked, that the manner in which the sensation renders these differences of the stimuli is quite peculiar to itself. The difference in pitch between two tones has no similarity at all to the difference of two numbers, but expresses an altogether peculiar increment of qualitative intensity, which by no means admits of being divined beforehand, and of which we have elsewhere no example. Just so the distinguished instance of a doubling of the number of waves finds an expression peculiar to it, in the octave, which is not experienced in sensation as a doubling of anything whatever, but as a noteworthy and otherwise unexampled combination of the identity and difference of both tones. Colors, on the contrary, although in their prismatic arrangement they originate from a similar ascending scale of the number of waves, do not by any means arrange themselves for the immediate impression into a series of increasing pitch. This is dependent on the fact, that we can rightly expect a proportionality to exist only between the sensations and the neural processes as their proximate conditions. But we have no acquaintance with these latter; and on this account we compare, without reaching any comprehensive result, the sensations with the external stimuli on which they do not immediately depend.

Finally, since our sensations do not constitute a closed system, the thought is possible that the realm of the sensible is not exhausted by our senses; on the contrary, that there are other animal souls, with kinds of sensation quite different and yet — as is natural — wholly unknown to us.

§ 6. The duration of sensation can be compared as a gross magnitude with the duration of the neural process which excited it. For we find that under ordinary circumstances it is never longer than the duration of the external stimulus, unless this latter leaves behind permanent after-effects, either outside of or within us, which themselves in turn become stimuli for new sensations.

Strictly taken, an excitation of the nerve which has once originated can never cease of itself, but must be annulled by efficient counteracting forces. This customarily takes place; and, when the vitality is sound, it takes place by means of the ceaseless activity of the whole process of metabolism, by which constantly the nerve's normal condition of equilibrium is re-established, and thus rendered capable of an impartial reception of new impressions.

Such recovery, however, fails to take place with sufficient speed, not merely when the stimuli are of very great strength, but particularly in the sense of sight as a rule; and, in such a case, the well-known *after-images* correspond to the excitation which still continues to be kept up, and which sometimes even undergoes again a periodical increase. By 'after-images' is meant actual sensations which, if they are lively enough, make the organ of sense incapable of the reception of new impressions; — as, for example, the dazzling images which follow looking at the sun.

§ 7. Certain experiences of every-day occurrence — for example, the observation of a light approaching, or of a tone dying away — prove that we are in general very sensitive to minute differences in the intensity of the stimuli of sense. But this remains a mere matter of degree, greater or less; and the moment never comes when we could say that according to the measure afforded by immediate impression, one light is half as bright, or one tone twice as loud, as another.

The above-mentioned circumstance prevents us from discovering in the shortest way the exact law in accordance with which the sensation depends on the strength of the stimulus. It is true that we can easily establish a series of stimuli whose different intensities admit of accurate measurement; but we are unable to assign to each of these values, on the ground of introspection, the strength of the sensation that belongs to it, in numerical terms; and, therefore, we are also unable to discover, from a comparison of these two sets of values, the universal law which satisfies them all. We are therefore compelled to employ the following circuitous method.

That is to say, it happens sometimes, although rarely, that we are uncertain whether two impressions, α and β, are at all different and not rather of equal intensity. Now since in any case, in order that they may appear *different* at all, the stimulus which forms the basis of one must be greater or less than the stimulus to which the other corresponds, the question may be raised in the next place: How large must be the difference between two stimuli (a and b) of the same kind, in order that the two sensations (α and β) corresponding to them may appear 'just observably different'? and further: Is this difference of the stimuli (b–a), which is the necessary condition of such transition from the similarity of the sensations to the 'just observable difference' in their intensity, always the same, or does it alter with the increase of the absolute magnitude of the stimulus?

According to the fundamental investigations of Ernst Heinrich Weber, which have since been confirmed and extended by many others, two sensations are distinguished as *two* only in case the intensities of both the stimuli which occasion them stand in a definite geometrical relation. In other words: To a certain stimulus **a**, in order that the sensation **α**, first excited by it, may pass over into a sensation **β**, whose difference from the former is just observable, there must be joined an increment **x** which is so much the greater, the greater **a** itself already is.

This relation which **a** and **b** (or, respectively, **a** and **x**) must sustain to the result in question, remains the same for the sensations of one and the same sense; but, of course, only within the limits between stimuli of too small intensity, which do not excite the nerve, and those of too great intensity, which disturb its function. On the contrary, it is different for different senses: — approximately about 3 : 4 for hearing and for mere sensations of pressure on the skin; 15 : 16 for the latter, in case they are supplemented (when the weights are lifted) by muscular feeling; 100 : 101 for sensations of light.

§ 8. This dependence of our capacity for making distinctions upon the relation, in respect of magnitudes, of the stimuli, which has been directly derived from the observations, forms the content of the so-called "Law of Weber."

In all the foregoing the question remains as yet wholly undecided, *in what way* precisely this relation in the magnitudes of the stimuli makes us capable of distinguishing the resulting impressions: that is to say, whether it is due to the fact that stimuli of different intensity produce an observably different intensity of the sensation, while its kind remains wholly unchanged; or whether it is due to the fact that different 'intensities' of the same stimulus beget qualitatively different sensations, which are then separated by us just according to their differences of quality.

In itself considered, every sensation is a single indivisible act. Now it is undoubtedly permissible for us to separate in thought, as two constituent parts of this act, the qualitative content and the intensity with which this content is experienced; — this, so far as the immediate impression, which alone can decide the point, accords therewith. Such is, for example, the case with tones. Here we may actually convince ourselves that a tone of definite pitch and color of 'clang' can sound louder or weaker without, on that account, altering its nature. On the contrary, it is very questionable whether the sensation of a pressure of greater intensity is really the *same* sensation as that of a smaller intensity, except that the former is stronger than the latter; further, whether the taste of a concentrated acid is really the same taste as that of the dilute acid. Much more repugnant still is immediate feeling toward our considering cold as merely a weaker intensity of heat. Both are rather at opposite poles, although the causes of their production are similar processes. Finally, different intensities of light actually have likewise different shades of colors; a white of a less intensity of brightness is not merely so, but it has become a gray, and this gray, as well as the black, which is the last result, cannot possibly be regarded as merely a feebler sensation of the white.

The foregoing considerations have hitherto not been sufficiently regarded; and neither have they been refuted. What further is now to be adduced depends upon an assumption which is perhaps correct but which is unproved: namely, that sensations become distinguishable because their intensities vary according to a fixed standard.

§ 9. We have, then, in the first place, to recognize the truth that there must be a certain small magnitude of stimulus for each sense, below which it cannot fall if any sensation whatever is to originate. Naturally enough, some resistance, by which the stimuli of too small intensity are kept from an influence on the soul, is assumed in order to explain the above-mentioned circumstance, which is by no means a matter of course. But where such resistance is achieved, as it were, is not known.

It is further assumed, that the transition from complete likeness or unobservable difference between two impressions to a difference just observable is always one and the same constant increment of the intensity of the sensation (that is, of the second impression compared with that of the first); and, accordingly, the fineness of the distinctions may be employed as a measure for the intensity of the sensations.

The question may then be asked: How must the stimuli increase, in order that the transition from one of its values to another may invariably result in the same constant increment of the intensity of the sensation?

According to the investigations already referred to, the foregoing question is answered as follows: If the intensities of the sensation are to increase by a constant difference, and therefore in an *arithmetical* series, the intensities of the stimuli must be augmented much more rapidly, that is, in a *geometrical* series. Or — what is the same thing — the relation of the first to the second is comparable to the relation of a logarithm to the number of which it is the logarithm. More simply expressed; the sensation belongs to those achievements or activities which are always to be raised to a higher degree with the more difficulty the greater the intensity with which they are already in exercise.

The following questions, however, still remain to be answered:—

(1) Why does this peculiar relation take place at all; and why does not the sensation rather (a thing which would be much more natural) increase as a simple proportional of the stimulus? None of the theories proposed on this point is satisfactory; but still the most probable is the assumption that, in the transformation of the external stimulus into excitations of the nerves, something or other occurs which causes the latter to augment much more slowly than the external stimuli increase.

(2) But how does it come about that, while the stimulus constantly augments in intensity, the intensity of the sensation increases not merely in a much smaller degree but also only discontinuously? Why are not, as a rule, all the impressions distinguished as different? How does it come about that, for

example, a weight 3 must increase to at least 4 in order to give a new sensation of pressure; that, on the contrary, it gives no such sensation, if it is only $3\frac{1}{4}$, $3\frac{1}{2}$, $3\frac{3}{4}$? Something in itself impossible is involved in the thought that a force which increases constantly should, nevertheless, furnish the occasion for a second kind of action only by sudden increments or discontinuously; and if not thus, then not at all. There are, then, doubtless contrivances conceivable, by means of which this discontinuity of the sensation could be produced. But we have not the least information as to where or how, in the body or in the soul, such contrivances do in fact exist.

Both these riddles are therefore wholly unsolved.

§ 10. It may perhaps be asserted that a state of rest, or an excitation maintained with complete uniformity, is never the proximate condition of a sensation; but that such condition is always nothing but the transition from one state to another.

It would follow from the foregoing that sensations, such as we might have last during a considerable time, — for example, the seeing of a light or the hearing of a tone, — must depend on certain series of single impulses with intervening pauses; so that in this case also a frequent repetition of the alternation between excitation and non-excitation would take place. For sensations of light and sound this admits of being established by proof. In these cases, to be sure, every single flash of light, or every tone however brief, depends upon a considerable number of such discrete impulses which are carried to the organ of sense. As to the rest of the senses we lack information.

Now if the above-mentioned fact is expressed as follows, — that all processes of excitation which are to lead to sensations must have this form of oscillation between two opposite states, — then we must at least not add the statement that the sensation itself consists in the *recounting*, as it were, of these single impulses. In these impulses we can never see anything but the matter-of-fact condition to which the originating of the sensation is attached in an incomprehensible way. For in the content of the sensation itself, in the red or the warm, we perceive nothing of motions whatever; and still less of the number of their oscillations, by means of which they become the causes of sensation.

§ **11.** If the same excitation **a**, which is customarily effected in a nerve by an external stimulus, and upon which the sensation α follows, is exceptionally produced by a stimulus originated in the interior of the body; then the same sensation a follows as well. In such a case the sensation is called *subjective*. Common. examples are ringing in the ears, flashes of light before the eyes, the chill and flush of fever.

In connection with this, the so-called principle of the "Specific Energy of the Nerves" has been laid down, according to which every individual nerve of sense, by whatsoever means it may have been excited, always produces the same sensation.

If the fact were such, it would not be very wonderful. For every coherent system of parts, which is disturbed but not destroyed, enters upon efforts at the re-establishment of its equilibrium, the form of which depends solely upon its own structure and upon the connection of the forces effective in it; and such system is not altered according to the variety of the disturbing stimuli. But in order that these efforts in the one nerve may be distinguished from those in every other, each nerve must have its own special structure,—a matter of which we as yet know nothing.

There are no facts, however, such as it is intended to explain in this way. We merely know that the stimulus of light, impact and pressure, the passage of a current of electricity through the eye, awaken the sensation of light; and perhaps that impact and electricity produce also the sensation of sound; and the latter also the sensation of taste. Now a motion of the ponderable parts by means of impact can scarcely take place in the tense eye-ball without a part of this motion being also converted into motions of the ether that exists in the eye, and so producing a motion of light, which acts as adequate stimulus upon the nerve of sight in precisely the same way as if it came from without. Just so the imparted shocks may be changed into oscillations of the tense parts and membranes, which are then normal stimuli for the nerve of hearing just as well as are the acoustic waves that come from without. Finally, it is quite certain that the electrical current excites chemical decomposition of the fluids of the mouth, and that the adequate stimulus for the nerve of taste consists in this directly. It is still possible to make the following assertion: In order that a nerve may be thrown into the state **a**, upon which the sensation *α* follows, a definite adequate stimulus is always necessary; but very many inadequate stimuli, in case of their being of influence, divide into different components: one of these components is then the adequate stimulus which is the condition of the sensation *α*; and the others become objects of perception through other sensations (for example, the pain contemporaneous with the impact).

§ 12. The influence of the external stimuli does not take place in so simple a manner as was formerly supposed; in such manner, for example, that the waves of light immediately as such act upon the nerve of sight and, in accordance with their nature, awaken all possible sensations of color and light. Instead of this we find in the eye certain layers of a peculiar, and still in many respects mysterious, structure (layers of rods and cones), which seem designed to transform the motion of light that reaches them into a chemical alteration of a special substance (visual purple) which, in turn, acts as the primary stimulus upon the nerve of sight. Just so do we find in the skin, and in the tongue, peculiarly constructed corpuscles of touch and corpuscles of taste, which first give to the stimulus, in a manner as yet unknown, the form in which it is to act upon the nerves contained in them.

In the organ of hearing we do not know of anything similar. For its purpose, however, another form of contrivance seems to have been hit upon, so that each single nerve-fibre is susceptible only for a single tone. The entire expansion of the fibres (upon the organ of Corti) would therefore be comparable to the key-board of a piano, and each fibre accessible only to a definite rate of the vibration of the waves.

The phenomena of 'color-blindness' have led to a similar hypothesis in relation to the eye. It is supposed that there are three species of fibres, each of which, when stimulated by itself alone, causes the sensation of one of the three fundamental colors, — green, red, and violet. From the synchronous excitation of the fibres of different species the other colors are then supposed to arise. This hypothesis is not invented gratuitously; but, as was just said, it has a reference to the facts of color-blindness, which it is designed to explain. The further demand, however, must not be made, — namely, to see into the reason why a definite mixture of synchronous excitations from red, green, and violet, causes the other colors, like blue and yellow, to originate; when the latter, so far as the mere immediate impression of sensation is concerned, do not in the least degree appear deducible from the former.

§ **13.** In another meaning of the words, *all* our sensations are only 'subjective'; that is to say, only phenomena in our consciousness, to which nothing in the external world corresponds. Even in antiquity this assertion was made; modern physics further completes the picture. The world outside of us is neither still nor resonant, neither bright nor dark; but it is as utterly incomparable to all that as sweetness is, for example, to a line. Nothing happens outside of us but motions of various forms. Finally, physiology often expresses the fact in the following inapt terms. Sensations are merely perceptions of our own states. But what takes place in the nerves while we are seeing, we do not at all perceive; and a state which, within our own soul, precedes the sensation in such a way that the latter could be designated as the perception of it, is also unknown to us. We can therefore simply say: Sensations are phenomena in us which, although they are the consequences of external stimuli, are not copies of them.

The proofs, however, by means of which the effort is ordinarily made to establish the foregoing principle, all admit of still other subterfuges. It would still always be possible to assume, that 'Things' *are* actually red or sweet, but that we could of course only *know* this in case they caused motions to act upon us; which motions — to be sure — are neither red nor sweet, and yet in the last result cause to originate in our soul, *as sensations*, the same redness and sweetness which belong as properties to the Things. The only proof, in the last analysis, consists in this, that such *objective* properties are in themselves inconceivable. In what the shining of a light which absolutely no one were to see, or the sounding of a tone which no one were to hear, could consist, is just as impossible to tell, as what a tooth-ache, which no one were to have, would be.

It is therefore involved in the nature of colors, tones, smells, etc., that they always have only *one* place and *one* way where and how they can by any possibility exist,—namely, the consciousness of a soul; and, of course, only at the moment when they are experienced by this soul.

CHAPTER II.

THE COURSE OF IDEAS.

§ 14. 'Ideas,' in contrast to 'sensations,' is the name primarily given to those images of memory arising from previous sensations, with which we meet in consciousness. This accords with the usage of speech; we form an idea of what is absent, of what we do not perceive by sense; but we perceive by sense what is present,—that of which, on just that very account, we do not need to form an idea. Ideas have their peculiar differences from sensations. The idea of the brightest radiance does not shine, that of the intensest noise does not sound, that of the greatest torture produces no pain; while all this is true, however, the idea quite accurately represents the radiance, the sound, or the pain, which it does not actually reproduce.

§ 15. Even in the aforesaid form the images of memory derived from earlier impressions are not *always* present in consciousness, but only temporarily return in it; and then in such manner that no external stimulus was necessary in order to produce them anew.

From the foregoing facts we conclude, that meantime our ideas have not been wholly lost to us, but have been transformed into some kind of 'unconscious states,' of which we, of course, can give no description, and for which we employ the self-contradictory but convenient name of 'unconscious ideas,' in order to indicate that they have originated from ideas and, under certain conditions, can become such again. A theory of the so-called 'course of ideas' would have to explain both the above-mentioned events.

§ **16.** The vanishing of ideas out of consciousness no one can observe: concerning this matter we can speak only on the ground of conclusions from what we subsequently find in consciousness, or on the ground of very general principles.

Here two views stand opposed to each other. It was formerly held that the vanishing of the ideas is natural, and the opposite of this, memory, was believed to need explanation. The analogy of the physical law of inertia is now followed, and forgetfulness is believed to need explanation, because of itself the eternal continuance of a state once excited is a self-evident affair.

The foregoing analogy is not without weight. It is true of the motion of bodies. But motion is only a change of external relations, from which the body moved suffers nothing, for it exists in one place exactly as well as in another; and it has therefore neither a reason nor a standard for offering resistance to the motion. The soul, on the contrary, exists in different inner states, according as it has the idea **a**, or the idea **b**, or no idea at all. It would therefore be conceivable that it should react against each impression that is obtruded upon it, and should by this means perhaps have the power to transform this impression from a conscious sensation into an unconscious state, although never, of course, the power of annulling it.

The other principle, too, which in itself considered is certainly to be recognized, — namely, that it is the unity of the soul, which necessitates the many ideas to reciprocal action in such manner that some of them supplant the others, — does not lead us to the desired end. For if the question is raised, In what way then shall this unity of the soul make itself felt upon the manifoldness of the ideas? — then the most probable conjecture would be this, that it fuses all the qualitatively different sensations or ideas into a single homogeneous intermediate state. This does not happen, however; but the ideas, — for example, 'gold' and 'blue' or 'large' and 'small,' — which have once arisen as different in consciousness, are never afterward intermingled. It is also obvious that every higher spiritual production, which consists essentially in relations between different points of relation, would be impossible, if the difference in the points to be related were made to vanish through being thus thrown together into a single mixed state.

Nothing else is therefore left for us but to consider the following thoughts as mere hypotheses which are not deducible from first principles.

§ 17. In accordance with the analogy of physical mechanics, the ideas are considered as 'forces' which act on each other according to the measure of their 'opposition' and their 'intensity.' Both parts of this hypothesis are scarcely to be established on grounds of experience.

In the first place, as to what concerns the intensity, this conception is certainly applicable to *sensations;* and, indeed, in such a manner that the greater content of the sensation is at all times a greater achievement of the activity of sensation, or a greater commotion and affection of the sentient subject. But the bare idea of a bright lustre is no greater achievement of the ideating activity than that of a dull glimmer; and that of thunder demands no greater exertion of this activity than that of the slightest whisper. The ideating activity therefore appears in general to admit of no differences in intensity, but such differences appertain wholly to the content of the idea.

Even the more or less 'obscure' ideas, which we think we have of one and the same content, produce no different intensity in the ideating act. Simple ideas, which we believe we have only 'obscurely,'—for example, that of the taste of a rare fruit,—we do not have at all; but we merely know from another source that the fruit has some taste. Now the greater the scope within the limits of which we are able to choose between different tastes, yet without knowing how to make a decision, the more obscure does the idea of the actual taste appear to us, which we are merely seeking for, but do not possess. Composite ideas, such as images of external objects or scientific principles, do not become 'obscure' by their entire content being gradually more weakly illuminated; but they thus become incomplete. Single factors fail wholly; but especially are those definite combinations forgotten, in which the yet remaining factors or points of relation stand. Again, the greater is the throng of possible connections between which we are wavering in our uncertainty; so much the greater is the so-called obscurity of the aforesaid ideas. Conversely, as soon as an idea is thought of completely, with all its content and all the combinations of its parts, it is then no longer possible mentally to represent it with a greater or less degree of intensity. Only it appears to receive a further increment of clearness, — for example, the idea of a triangle, — in case a throng of other thoughts are connected therewith in the experience of an expert, which are still unknown to the beginner.

§ 18. The other conception applicable in this place, that of *opposition*, also awakens the inquiry, whether it is to be referred to the content of the ideas or to the activities by which they are mentally represented.

The two things are not coincident. Ideas in general, never *are*, of themselves, that which they *signify*: the idea of what is red is not a red idea; the idea of what is triangular is not triangular; the idea of what is choleric is not choleric. If, therefore, the contents of two ideas, — like 'right' and 'left,' 'plus' and 'minus,' 'white' and 'black,' — are opposed to each other, it does not in the least degree follow from this, that the ideating activities by which they are produced as ideas are opposed to each other in the same way; and that they must on this account, as a matter of course, hinder each other, after the analogy of opposed physical motions or forces.

§ 19. Moreover, the conceptions of intensity and opposition could serve as a foundation for a 'psychical mechanics,' in a self-evident way, only in case they should have reference to the ideating activities. This is not the case.

If therefore the intensity and opposition of the content ideated were the decisive conditions for the reciprocal action of the ideas, we should be compelled to recognize it as a bare fact. Experience does not establish this. The idea of a greater content by no means always supplants that of the smaller; on the contrary, the latter itself is sometimes in a position to suppress the sensation from external stimuli.

But ideas never make their appearance in a soul which does nothing else besides; on the contrary, there is also connected with every impression, a somewhat that is represented in idea in consequence of this, — namely, a feeling of the value which the impression has for the bodily and spiritual well-being of the percipient. Such feelings of pleasure and pain are just as obviously capable of a gradation of degrees as the bare act of mental representation is incapable of this. Now according to the magnitude of this proportion of feeling, which is moreover extraordinarily changeable according to the variety of the total condition in which the soul is at the time,—or, briefly said, according to the degree of the interest which an idea is, for manifold reasons, able to awaken at each moment,—its greater or less power is directed toward the supplanting of other ideas. And it is only in this, and not in an original property which it might be supposed to possess as a mere idea, that what may be called its '*intensity*' consists.

§ 20. The second question (§ 15) was this: How do ideas return in consciousness?

On this point we merely know that an idea **b** very often returns in case another idea **a** has been produced in consciousness.

Now however, since it is not every **b** that returns in consequence of any **a** we please, there must be a closer connection between those which do in this way recall each other, than between those which do not. Such connection is called 'Association';—a mere name which does not in the least express by what means the connection is established. In the same way 'Reproduction' is a mere name for the fact that a definite **a** brings back again into consciousness some **b** associated with it.

But, nevertheless, the conditions can be studied under which both, association and reproduction, as a matter of fact take place.

The two classes customarily adduced first, according to which similar ideas on the one hand, and opposed ideas on the other hand, recall each other, it is found difficult to establish by experience. For it cannot well be said, that a tone or a color recalls to remembrance all other tones and colors in a more lively way than it recalls any other ideas whatever. If, on the other hand, things opposed,—like darkness to light, night to day, plus to minus,—cause each other to be thought of, the reason does not lie in such opposition alone, but in the special value which it has for our life or for particular employments, so that we are on this account reminded by one of the other.

On the contrary, it is quite certain that the third and fourth cases do occur; according to which, on the one hand, each part of a space-whole reproduces the remaining parts and the whole, and, on the other hand, the parts of a successive whole—for example, a melody—recall each other following their original order. Examples are unnecessary. It also appears unnecessary to reduce the third case, as is frequently done, to the fourth, because (as is said) even the perception of a simultaneous whole happens after all in the way of a succession; since the eye with its glance runs over the forms and gradually becomes conscious of the connection of each point with the next. We certainly do attain *accurate* mental images only in the aforesaid manner; still it is not to be denied that even an instantaneous apprehension of mental images can be left behind, the single parts of which will reproduce each other.

We may therefore summarize all the facts in the following way: Every two ideas, whatever their content may be, become associated in case they are produced either simultaneously or immediately (that is, without any intermediate member) following each other. And upon this fact would be founded with out further technicality the special facility with which we repeat a number of ideas according to their series but not outside of the series.

Finally, if we designate as a special case the 'immediate' reproduction with which **a** is again awakened by the influence of a new stimulus that produces the same **a**, then we are to consider that the second **a** could not be distinguished at all from the first as a repetition of it, if both were *completely* alike. But the first, which is re-awakened by the second, reproduces in its turn the idea of the concomitant circumstances under which it was previously perceived; and these are different from the circumstances of the present moment. Therefore the recognition of the same **a** depends after all on 'mediated' reproduction, — that is, reproduction of other ideas *through* **a**.

§ **21.** In the case of most ideas, each has become associated in the course of life with very many others in the same way. If, therefore, a definite **f** has returned again in consciousness, it still remains quite undecided which of the many other ideas, **g**, **h**, **i**, **k**, has just now reproduced it, since it was previously connected with them all. The grounds for the decision of this point will generally lie, partly in the course which the ideas before **f** have taken, and into the connection of which **g**, **h**, **i**, **k**, do not all fit equally well; partly in our common feeling or the mood in which we are at each moment as respects the vitality or the restraints of our whole existence; and finally, partly in special conditions of our corporeal life, that are to be altogether excluded from this part of the discussion, but of which we shall speak later on.

The foregoing points of view only admit of being brought forward in a general way. On the contrary, it is impossible to form a theory from them which enters into particulars; and just as impossible in any single case really to demonstrate the reasons which have in fact led to the course of our thoughts, appearing often so capricious as it does.

CHAPTER III.

THE ACT OF RELATIVE KNOWLEDGE AND ATTENTION.

§ **22.** Thus far we have spoken of the relations and interchange of ideas. There is in our interior life, however, besides this, a *mental representation* of these relations and of this interchange.

The two are very different things. We know that if the idea of 'blue,' and at the same time that of red, originates within us, the two by no means mingle and produce 'violet.' Were this, however, to happen, then a third simple idea would merely have taken the place of the two others, and a comparison of these two would have been made impossible by their vanishing. Every comparison, and in general every relation between two elements (in this case, red and blue), presupposes that both points of relation remain separate, and that an ideating activity passes over from the one **a** to the other **b**, and at the same time becomes conscious of that alteration which it has experienced in this transition from the act of forming the idea of **a** to that of forming **b**.

Such an activity do we exercise in case we compare red and blue; and thereupon there originates in us the new idea of a qualitative similarity which we ascribe to both.

If at the same time a strong and a weak light are perceived, then the sensation therefrom is not that of a single light which might be the sum of both; both rather remain separate; and again on passing from one to the other, we become conscious of another alteration in our state, — namely, that of the merely quantitative more or less of one and the same impression.

Finally, if two quite similar impressions have been able to originate as distinct ideas within us, then they no longer fuse into a third; but when we compare them in the foregoing way and, on the transition from one to the other, become conscious of no alteration of our mental representation, the new idea of '*Likeness*' originates in our minds.

§ **23.** It is important to make it obvious that all these new ideas, which we may designate as ideas of a higher order, by no means arise as resultants from a mere reciprocal action of the original simple ideas, in the same way as a third motion is constructed in mechanics from the coincidence of two others.

The foregoing analogy by no means holds good in the spiritual domain. The rather are both the impressions **a** and **b** always to be regarded merely as stimuli, that act upon the *entire* peculiar and 'monadic' nature of an ideating subject, and stir up as a reaction in this subject the activity by means of which the new ideas, — for example, of similarity, likeness, contrast, etc., — originate; nor would such ideas, without the excitation of this new spiritual activity, originate from the mere co-working of the single impressions.

§ **24.** In the same manner as the aforesaid new ideas does all that originate which we designate as 'general notions.'

It is customary to assert that those factors of the ideas compared, which are of unlike kind, annul each other by their opposition, and that the remainder which is of like kind then, of itself alone, exhibits the so-called "general" factor.

But the single examples from which we form a general notion by no means perish thereupon; on the contrary, their ideas continue to maintain themselves side by side with the general one, which is merely added to them as a new product. The general notion also never constitutes anything which admits of being mentally represented in intuitive form, as a definite image, in the same way as do the individual examples from which it originated. Thus 'color in general' is not representable by an idea; it looks neither green nor red, but has no look whatever. And just so there is no definite and fixed mental image whatever of animal in general, having an intuitive character similar to the image of each individual species of animal.

All such general notions, therefore, are not products of a coöperation of many individual ideas; for in that case they would have the same character as do these their components. The names by which we designate them — for example, 'colors' — are, strictly speaking, nothing more than demands made upon us mentally to represent a series of different individual impressions; though with the adjunct thought that what is contained in them belongs not to them, but to what they have in common, and yet does not admit of being separated from them as an idea of like kind.

§ 25. The different narrower and broader meanings of the term *Consciousness* are connected with the foregoing subject.

It often happens that we perceive a multiplicity of elements, but still do not at the instant know how to specify the definite relations between them. On the other hand, it is possible subsequently to become conscious of the relations, after the aforesaid sensuous impressions are already past. It follows from this that these impressions themselves are by no means *unconscious;* otherwise they would not subsequently be remembered. On the contrary, the relating activity of the mind, which enumerates them and also mentally represents the relations that actually exist between them, has not been exercised.

We see from this that the two operations are separable from each other: the relating activity can never originate as a higher form without the simple conscious sensation to which it is related; but the latter, as the lower form, does not need to be accompanied by the former.

Ordinary experiences show that there are very many circumstances which hinder the appearance of this higher activity. In the case of manifold movements of the mind, we hear the tones but do not understand the words; or understand the words but not their meaning; or, finally, this too, but nothing of the significance which it has for our interests. Even bodily conditions, of which we yet know almost nothing, bring it about that the matter stops with the mere sensation of impressions: and neither their external and intuitive, nor their interior, connection comes into consciousness ('*soul-blindness*').

§ 26. What we have here depicted is, fundamentally considered, nothing else but the series of different degrees of *Attention.*

This was formerly considered as an activity exercised by the spirit, which, like a light waxing and waning, illumines to greater clearness the of themselves unconscious impressions. Later (Herbart) this thought of an activity has been wholly abandoned: and it has been supposed that the sentence, "we are attentive to something," only signifies: The idea of this something rises into our consciousness by its own strength.

We cannot accede to this latter assumption; but just as little do we understand attention to be merely a stronger illumination of a given content. By attention we gain something merely in case the content mentally represented gives occasion for its work to our relating and comparing faculty of knowledge. Even an altogether simple content is at least compared by us with other simple contents, or with itself at different moments of its duration. If we disregard this fact, then the mere persistence of the content, with whatever intensity it may occur, is of absolutely no help to us.

It is understood, finally, that this relation of one content to another can be carried further at pleasure. We can therefore certainly distinguish yet other different degrees of consciousness concerning the content of an idea; — and this according as we mentally represent merely the idea itself and its own nature, or its connection with other ideas, or, finally, its value and significance for the totality of our personal life.

CHAPTER IV.

THE INTUITIONS OF SPACE.

§ **27.** Metaphysic raises the doubt, whether space is actually extended and we, together with 'Things,' are contained in it; whether — just the reverse — the whole spatial world is not rather only a form of intuition in us.

This question we for the present leave one side, and in the meantime take our point of departure from the assumption, previously alluded to, with which we are all conversant. But since Things in space can never become the object of our perception by virtue of their bare existence, and, on the contrary, become such solely through the effects which they exercise upon us, the question arises: How do the Things by their influence upon us bring it to pass, that we are compelled mentally to represent them in the same reciprocal position in space, in which they actually exist outside of us?

§ **28.** In the case of the eye, nature has devised a painstaking structure, such that the rays of light which come from a luminous point are collected again at one point on the retina, and that the different points of the image, which originate here, assume the same reciprocal relation toward one another as the points of the object outside of us, to which they correspond. Without doubt, this so-called 'image of the object,' so carefully prepared, is an indispensable condition of our being able mentally to present the object in its true form and position. But it is the source of all the errors in this matter, to believe that the bare existence of this image, without anything else, explains our idea of the position of its parts. The entire image is essentially nothing but a representative of the external object, transposed into the interior of the organ of sense; and how we know and experience aught of it, is now just as much the question as the question previously was, — How can we perceive the external object?

§ 29. If one wished to conceive of the soul itself as an extended being, then the impressions on the retina would, of course, be able to transplant themselves, with all their geometrical regularity, to the soul. One point of the soul would be excited as green, the other red, a third yellow; and these three would lie at the corners of a triangle precisely in the same way as the three corresponding excitations on the retina.

It is also obvious, however, that there is no real gain in all this. The bare fact that three different points of the soul are excited is, primarily, a disconnected three-fold fact. A knowledge thereof, however, and therefore a knowledge of this three-foldness, and of the reciprocal positions of the three points, is, nevertheless, by no means given in this way: but such knowledge could be brought about only by means of a uniting and relating activity; and this itself, like every activity, would be perfectly foreign to all predicates of extension and magnitudes in space.

§ 30. The same thought is more immediately obvious if we surrender this useless notion of the soul being extended, and consider it as a supersensible essence, which, in case we wish to bring it at all into connection with spatial determinations, could be represented only as an indivisible point.

On making the transition into this indivisible point, the manifold impressions must obviously lose all the geometrical relations which they might still have upon the extended retina, — just in the same way as the rays of light, which converge at the single focus of a lens, are not side by side with one another, but only all together, in this point. Beyond the focus, the rays diverge in the same order as that in which they entered it. Nothing analogous to this, however, happens in our consciousness; that is to say, the many impressions, which were previously side by side with one another, do not actually again separate from each other; but, instead of this, the aforesaid activity of mental presentation simply occurs, and it transposes their images to different places in the space that is only 'intuited' by it.

Here, too, the previous observation holds good: The mental presentation *is* not that which it presents; and the idea of a point on the left does not lie on the left of the idea of a point on the right; but of one mental presentation, which in itself has no spatial properties whatever, both points are merely themselves so presented before the mind, as though one lay to the left, the other to the right.

§ **31.** The following result now stands before us: Many impressions exist conjointly in the soul, although not spatially side by side with one another; but they are merely together in the same way as the synchronous tones of a chord; that is to say, qualitatively different, but not side by side with, above or below, one another. Notwithstanding, the mental presentation of a spatial order must be produced again from these impressions. The question is, therefore, in the first place, to be raised: How in general does the soul come to apprehend these impressions, not in the form in which they actually are, — to wit, non-spatial, — but as they are not, in a spatial juxtaposition?

The satisfactory reason obviously cannot lie in the impressions themselves, but must lie solely in the nature of the soul in which they appear, and upon which they themselves act simply as stimuli.

On this account, it is customary to ascribe to the soul this tendency to form an intuition of space, as an originally inborn capacity. And indeed we are compelled to rest satisfied with this. All the 'deductions' of space, hitherto attempted, which have tried to show on what ground it is necessary to the nature of the soul to develop this intuition of space, have utterly failed of success. Nor is there any reason to complain over this matter; for the simplest modes of the experience of the soul must always merely be recognized as given facts, — just as, for example, no one seriously asks why we only hear, and do not rather taste, the waves of air.

§ **32.** The second question is much more important. Let it be assumed that the soul once for all lies under the necessity of mentally presenting a certain manifold as in juxtaposition in space; How does it come to localize every individual impression at a definite place in the space intuited by it, in such manner that the entire image thus intuited is similar to the external object which acted on the eye?

Obviously, such a clue must lie in the impressions themselves. The simple quality of the sensation 'green' or 'red' does not, however, contain it; for every such color can in turn appear at every point in space, and on this account does not, of itself, require always to be referred to the one definite point.

We now remind ourselves, however, that the carefulness with which the regular position on the retina of the particular excitations is secured, cannot be without a purpose. To be sure, an impression is not *seen* at a definite point on account of its *being situated* at such point; but it may perhaps by means of this definite situation *act* on the soul otherwise than if it were elsewhere situated.

Accordingly we conceive of this in the following way: Every impression of color **r** — for example, red — produces on all places of the retina, which it reaches, the same sensation of redness. In addition to this, however, it produces on each of these different places, **a**, **b**, **c**, a certain accessory impression, α, β, γ, which is independent of the nature of the color seen, and dependent merely on the nature of the place excited. This second local impression would therefore be associated with every impression of color **r**, in such manner that **rα** signifies a red that acts on the point **a**, **rβ** signifies the same red in case it acts on the point **b**. These associated accessory impressions would, accordingly, render for the soul the clue, by following which it transposes the same red, now to one, now to another spot, or simultaneously to different spots in the space intuited by it.

In order, however, that this may take place in a methodical way, these accessory impressions must be completely different from the main impressions, the colors, and must not disturb the latter. They must be, however, not merely of the same kind among themselves, but wholly definite members of a series or a system of series; so that for every impression **r** there may be assigned, by the aid of this adjoined 'local sign,' not merely a particular, but a quite definite spot among all the rest of the impressions.

§ 33. The foregoing is the theory of '*Local Signs.*' Their fundamental thought consists in this, that all spatial differences and relations among the impressions on the retina must be compensated for by corresponding non-spatial and merely intensive relations among the impressions which exist together without space-form in the soul; and that from them in reverse order there must arise, not a new actual arrangement of these impressions in extension, but only the mental presentation of such an arrangement in us. To such an extent do we hold this principle to be a necessary one.

On the contrary, only hypotheses are possible in order to answer the question, In what do those accessory impressions requisite consist, so far as the sense of sight is concerned? We propose the following conjecture:—

In case a bright light falls upon a lateral part of the retina, on which—as is well known—the sensitiveness to impressions is more obtuse than in the middle of the retina, then there follows a rotation of the eye until the most sensitive middle part of the retina, as the receptive organ, is brought beneath this light: we are accustomed to style this the "fixation of vision" upon the aforesaid light. Such motion happens involuntarily, without any original cognition of its purpose, and uniformly without cognition of the means by which it is brought about. We may therefore reckon it among the so-called reflex motions, which originate by means of an excitation of one nerve, that serves at other times for sensation, being transplanted to motor nerves without any further assistance from the soul and in accordance with the pre-existing anatomical connections; and these latter nerves being therefore stimulated to execute a definite motion in a perfectly mechanical way. Now in order to execute such a rotation of the eye as serves the purpose previously alluded to, every single spot in the retina, in case it is stimulated, must occasion a magnitude and direction of the aforesaid rotation peculiar to it alone. But at the same time all these rotations of the eye would be perfectly comparable motions, and, of course, members of a system of series that are graded according to magnitude and direction.

§ **34.** The application of the foregoing hypothesis (many more minute particular questions being disregarded) we conceive of as follows:—In case a bright light falls upon a lateral point **P** of a retina, which has not yet had any sensation of light whatever, then there arises, in consequence of the connection in the excitation of the nerves, such a rotation of the eye as that, instead of the place **P**, the place **E** of clearest vision is brought beneath the approaching stimulus of the light. Now while the eye is passing through the arc **PE**, the soul receives at each instant a feeling of its momentary position,—a feeling of the same kind as that by which we are, when in the dark, informed of the position of our limbs. To the arc **PE** there corresponds then a series of constantly changing feelings of position, the first member of which we call π, and the last of which we call ϵ.

If now, in a second instance, the place **P** is again stimulated by the light, then there originates not simply the rotation **PE** for a second time, but the initial member of the series of feelings of position, π, reproduces in memory the entire series associated with it, $\pi\epsilon$; and this series of mental presentations is independent of the fact that at the same time also the rotation of the eye **PE** actually follows.

Exactly the same thing would hold good of another point **R**; only the arc **RE**, the series of feelings $\rho\epsilon$, and also the initial member of the series, ρ, would have other values.

Now finally, in case it came about that both places, **P** and **R**, were simultaneously stimulated with an equal intensity, and that the arcs **PE** and **RE** were equal but in opposite directions to each other, then the actual rotation of the eye **PE** and **RE** could not take place; on the other hand, the excitation upon the places **P** and **R** is nevertheless not without effect; each reproduces the series of feelings of position belonging to it, — respectively, $\pi\epsilon$ and $\rho\epsilon$. Although therefore the eye does not now move, yet there is connected with every excitation of the places **P** and **R** the mental presentation of the magnitude and of the qualitative peculiarity of a series of changes, which consciousness or the common feeling would have to experience, in order that these excitations may fall upon the place of clearest vision, or, according to the customary expression, in the line of vision.

And now we assert that to see anything 'to the right' or 'to the left' of this line of vision means nothing more than this, to be conscious of the magnitude of the achievement which would be necessary to bring the object into this line.

§ 35. By the foregoing considerations nothing further would be established than the relative position of the single colored points in the field of vision. The entire image, on the contrary, would still have no place at all in a yet larger space; indeed, even the mental presentation of such a place would as yet have no existence.

Now this image first attains a place with reference to the eye, the repeated opening and closing of which, since it can become known to us in another way, is the condition of its existence or non-existence. That is to say, the visible world is *in front* before our eyes. What is behind us not merely has no existence whatever for us, but we do not once know that there is anything which should be called 'behind.'

The motions of the body lead us further. If the field of vision in a position of rest contains from left to right the images **abc**, and we then turn ourselves to the right upon our axis, **a** vanishes, but **d** appears on the right, and therefore the images **bcd, cde, def, . . . xyz, yza, zab, abc,** succeed in order. As a result of such recurrence of the images with which we began, the two following thoughts originate; namely, that the visible world of objects exists in a closed circuit of extension about us, and that the alteration of our own position, which we perceive by means of the changing feelings of position while turning, depends upon an alteration of our relation to this immovable world of objects, — that is to say, upon a *motion.*

It is easily understood that the mental picture of a spherical extension originates from the aforesaid mental picture of a closed horizon by means of repeatedly turning in a similar way in various other directions.

§ 36. But, nevertheless, this spherical surface also would always have only a superficial extension; no intimation would as yet exist of a *depth* to space.

Now the mental presentation, to the effect that something like a third dimension of space in general exists, cannot originate of itself, but only through the experience which we have in case we move about among the visible objects. From the manifold displacements which the particular visual images experience, in a manner that is tedious to describe but very easy to imagine, we gain the impression, that each line in an image originally seen is the beginning of new surfaces which do not coincide with that previously seen, but which lead out into this space, now extended on all sides, to greater or less distances from the line.

Another question to be treated subsequently is this: By what means do we estimate the different magnitudes of the distance into this depth of space?

§ **37.** The crossing of the rays of light in the narrow opening of the pupil is the cause of the image of the upper points of the object being formed beneath, that of the lower points above on the retina; and of the whole picture having therefore a position the reverse of the object. But it is a prejudice on this account to consider seeing in inverse position to be natural, and seeing in upright position to be mysterious. Like every geometrical property of the image, so this one of its position, too, on passing into consciousness, is completely lost; and the position in which we see things is in no way prejudiced by the aforesaid position of the image on the retina.

Now, however, in order that we may be able to ascribe to objects a position at all, in order therefore that the expressions 'above,' 'below,' 'upright,' and 'inverted,' may have a meaning, we must have, independent of all sensation by sight, a mental picture of a space in which the entire content of the field of vision shall be arranged, and in which 'above' and 'below' are two qualitatively opposite and, on this account, not exchangeable directions.

The muscular feeling affords us such a mental presentation. 'Below' is the place toward which the direction of gravity moves; 'above,' the opposite. Both directions are distinguished perfectly for us by means of an immediate feeling; and, on this account, we are never deceived even in the dark about the position and situation of our body.

Accordingly we see objects 'upright' in case the lower points of the object are reached by one and the same movement of the eyes simultaneously with those points of our own body which are 'below' according to the testimony of the aforesaid muscular feeling; and the upper points by a movement which, according to the same testimony, renders visible simultaneously the upper parts of our own selves.

Now it is exactly such agreement that is secured in *our* eye, in which the axis lies in front of the sensitive retina, by means of the inverted position of the retinal image. In an other eye, in which the sensitive surface should be placed in front of the axis, and yet the greatest sensitiveness also should appear in the middle portion of that surface, the retinal image would have to stand upright to serve the same purpose.

§ 38. The final and valid answer to the question, why we have single vision with two eyes, is not to be given. As is well known, it does not always happen. The rather must two impressions fall on two quite definite points of the retina in order to coalesce. We see double, on the contrary, if they fall on other points. Naturally, we shall say: The two places which belong together would have to impart like local signs to their impressions, and thereby render them indistinguishable; but we are not able to demonstrate in what manner this postulate is fulfilled. Physiology, too, in the last analysis, satisfies itself with a mere term for the fact; it calls 'identical' those places in both retinas which give one simple impression, and 'non-identical' those which give a double impression.

§ 39. Irritations of the skin we naturally refer at once to the place of the skin on which we see them acting. But in case of their repetition, when we are not able to see them, we have no assistance from remembering them; for the most ordinary stimuli have already in the course of our life touched all possible places of the skin, and could therefore now as well be referred to one place as to another. In order that they may be correctly localized, they would have at every instant to tell us anew where they belong; that is to say, there must be attached to the main impression (impact, pressure, heat or cold) an auxiliary impression which is independent of the latter and, on the contrary, dependent on the place of the skin that is irritated.

The skin can supply such local signs; for since it is connected without interruption, a single point of it cannot be irritated at all, without the surrounding portion experiencing a displacement, pulling, stretching, or concussion of some kind. But, further, since the skin possesses at different places a different thickness, different tension or liability to displacement, — extends sometimes above the firm surfaces of the bones, sometimes over the flesh of the muscles, sometimes over cavities; since, moreover, the members being manifold, these relations change from one stretch of skin to another; therefore the aforesaid sum of secondary effects around the point irritated will be different for each one from the remainder; and such effects, if they are taken up by the nerve-endings and act on consciousness, may occasion the feelings so difficult to describe, according to which we distinguish a contact at one place from the same contact at another.

It cannot be said, however, that each point of the skin has its special local sign. It is known from the investigations of E. H. Weber, that on the margin of the lips, the tip of the tongue, the tips of the fingers, being touched in two places (by the points of a pair of compasses) can be distinguished as two at an interval of only ½ line; while there are places on the arms, legs, and on the back, which require for making the distinction a distance between them of as much as 20 lines. We interpret this in the following way. Where the structure of the skin changes little for long stretches, the local signs also alter only a little from point to point. And if two stimuli act simultaneously, and accordingly a reciprocal disturbance of these secondary effects occurs, they will be undistinguishable; on the contrary, in cases where both stimuli act successively, and therefore the aforesaid disturbance ceases, both are still frequently distinguishable. On the other hand, we know nothing further to allege as to how the extraordinary sensitiveness — for example — of the lips is occasioned.

§ **40.** The preceding statement merely explains the possibility of distinguishing impressions made at different places; but each impression must also be referred to the definite place at which it acts.

This is easy for one who sees, since he already possesses a picture of the surface of his own body; and, on this account, he now by means of the unchanging local sign, even in the dark, translates each stimulus which he has once seen act on a definite place, to the same place in this picture of the body that is mentally presented before him. One born blind would be compelled to construct such a picture first by means of the sense of touch; and this naturally is accomplished through motions of the tactual members and by estimating the distances which they would have to travel in order to reach from contact at the point **a** to contact at the other point **b**. It is to be considered, however, that these motions — which in this case are not seen — are perceivable only by so-called muscular feelings; — that is to say, by feelings which in themselves are merely certain species of the way *we feel*, and do not of themselves at all indicate the motions which are in fact the causes of them.

Now it cannot be described, how it is that this interpretation of the muscular feelings actually originates in the case of those born blind; but the helps which lead to it are very probably found in the fact, that the sense of touch as well as the eye can receive many impressions simultaneously, and that, in case of a movement, the previous impression does not vanish without trace and have its place taken by a wholly new one; but, that, in the manner previously alleged, the combinations **abc**, **bcd**, etc., follow one another, and therefore some part in common is always left over for the next two impressions. By this alone does it seem possible to awaken the idea that the same occurrence, from which the series of changeable muscular feelings originates for us, consists in an alteration of our relation to a series of objects previously existent side by side and to be found arranged in a definite order; it consists, therefore, in a *motion.*

§ 41. It is questionable whether the mental picture of space which one born blind attains solely by the sense of touch will be altogether like that of one who sees; it is rather to be assumed that a much less intuitable system of mental presentations of time, of the magnitude of motion, and of the exertion which is needed in order to reach from contact at one point to that at another, takes the place of the clear, easy, and at once all-comprehending intuition, with which he who sees is endowed.

CHAPTER V.

OF THE APPREHENSION OF THE WORLD BY THE SENSES, AND OF ERRORS OF SENSE.

§ 42. A simple impression of sense represents only itself, and tells nothing concerning the 'Things' to which it belongs,—either as property, state, or action. This further interpretation is certainly, as the saying is, an affair of the *Understanding;* and it is the understanding that is deceived in case it permits itself to be led astray by means of a mental presentation **a,** which it previously, under secondary conditions (**c**) imperfectly apprehended, found combined with a presentation **b,** so as to think an **a,** when repeated under other conditions **d,** to be connected with the same **b.**

But the senses are not always so innocent. The eye, for example, when it pictures the world as extended in three dimensions on a plane, gives us absolutely false relations between the images of the single objects. In this case, therefore, in which sense yields what is false, while the intellect must furnish the corrections, we have a right to speak of "errors of sense." Under this class belong, for example, the incorrect diminishing of remote objects, the convergence of parallel lines in the distance, the elevation of the level of the sea above the coast, — pure phenomena which persist for the intuitions of sense, even after the intellect is no longer uncertain concerning the true state of affairs.

§ 43. The same magnitudes of space we estimate as greater when they are bright-colored; smaller, when they are dark. The surface filled with manifold objects appears larger to the eye; the empty one, smaller. To the sense of touch the rough surface appears larger than the smooth. In that direction which is made prominent by a manifold repetition of lines, things appear to extend farther than they actually do. All this is made use of in manifold ways by the decorative arts.

Distances we estimate (very indefinitely) as smaller for bright objects, larger for the dark ones; (much more accurately) as smaller so long as the interior delineation of things continues to be clear, larger in case it makes a confused impression as a whole.

We principally employ, however, three factors; the actual magnitude of a thing, its apparent magnitude, and the distance, in order from two of them to ascertain the third. If the true magnitude is given (for example, by our knowing that the object in question is a man or a child) and likewise the apparent magnitude, then we estimate the distance as so much the greater the smaller the second is in comparison with the first. If we know, besides the apparent magnitude, the distance, then we can reckon the actual magnitude in the same way. Finally, if we know the true magnitude and the distance, then we can find the apparent magnitude, which — for example — painting must give to the picture of an object, in order to make it appear at this distance. But where objects — for example, mountains and watercourses — have no natural measure, and therefore merely the apparent magnitude is given, we can make a conclusion with some accuracy to the actual magnitude and the distance *directly*, only by separating the latter into parts, and estimating each one of them according to the relation of the apparent magnitude of some well-known object found in them, to its true magnitude.

A very important means, finally, is the parallax, — that is to say, the magnitude of the displacement which the image of an object **C** experiences as seen against points definitely marked, **P, Q, R,** on an immovable background, in case we consider it from the two terminal points, **A** and **B,** of a line **AB.** It is greater for nearer, and smaller for more remote objects. We daily employ this means of assistance, since we fixate the object alternately with one eye or the other, or incline the head to the right and left, or actually move hither and thither. Science has made manifold use of this means, since it performs this experiment carefully and with the additional help of finer instruments of measurement.

§ **44.** The comparison of sensible qualities (colors, tones, tastes, degrees of heat) requires a certain moderateness of the impression, whether it be intensity, or extension in space, or duration in time. It requires, besides, that the testing organ be the same throughout, in order that the different local signs of different organs may not modify the impressions. Accordingly, we do not test the heat of two bodies of water with two fingers simultaneously, but successively with the same finger, etc. In such cases the other snare is to be shunned, — that of taking the interval too great to leave both impressions still lively enough in consciousness, or too small, so that the after-effects of the first impression are mingled with the second.

These after-effects are of a two-fold kind. If they are strong and recent, they obscure the second impression. But very frequently, and in different senses, the other result also occurs, — namely, that a nerve which has been for a considerable time thrown into the same one-sided excitation by an impression **a**, after the cessation of this stimulus, assumes of itself another form of excitation through which it returns to its impartial condition of equilibrium. These counter-excitations also produce sensations. Thus, for example, an eye that has been a long time busy with green, red, or yellow, subsequently sees the complementary colors, — red, green, and violet. In the domain of the sense of touch and of the muscular feeling, as well, these 'sensations of contrast' occur.

§ **45.** We hold an object to be *moved,* the image of which travels over our retina. And such an appearance takes place, not merely in case we are moving through the objects with a perfectly passive motion (for example, sailing on a vessel), but also in case we are moving through them in the consciousness of our actual motion and in the conviction that they are unmoved. Naturally the apparent motion of the objects has then the opposite direction to our own.

The well-known rotating motion, with which objects hasten by us after we have been for a long time rotating on the axis of our body and then immediately stand still, appears to have its basis in this, that the eyes unconsciously to ourselves still follow for some time the direction in which the body previously turned, and when they have reached the extreme angle of vision immediately turn back to begin anew the same course. Therefore it is always the same objects which ceaselessly pass by before us without vanishing from sight.

§ 46. In case some object or other (for example, a stick) is brought into a rather loose connection with our body (for example, the hand), such as admits of displacements of its position, then at each momentary position a new and special combination of sensations of pressure (for example, on the different fingers) is occasioned. In accordance with earlier experiences which we have had, we form for ourselves out of each such combination a mental picture of the position which the object (the stick) has at the moment. Now if it discovers in all positions the same resistance to an external object, and if also this pressure by the stick acts constantly on our hand, then we not only transfer the seat of this resistance to the common point of intersection of all these successive positions, but we believe with an altogether immediate perspicuity that we have a direct sensation of it at the spot where the resistance is accomplished, exactly as though we were just as much present, with our capacity for sensation, at the end of this stick, as in the surface of the hand where the other end of the stick is pressing.

These feelings of 'double contact,' which occur in almost innumerable examples, introduce into our mental presentations of external things a very peculiar life-likeness. Above all do they alone avail to make possible the serviceable use of many tools, — for example, probes, knifes, forks, pens; since we believe that by means of them we perceive the resistances or hinderances which these instruments find at the surface of their objects, quite directly *in loco;* and since we are able to apply the counter means that are each moment appropriate. They are further instructive concerning many properties of things, — for example, concerning the length of a balanced pole, concerning the breadth of a ladder-rung when stepped on, concerning the length of the thread fastened to which a ball is swung round in a circle. Finally, they give us in general the agreeable feeling of our spiritual presence being extended beyond the real limits of our body; and this is the reason for the many, in part elegant, and in part bizarre, movable additions or appendages to our bodies, of which the passion for dress is wont to avail itself.

CHAPTER VI.

THE FEELINGS.

§ **47.** We apply the name 'Feelings' exclusively to states of pleasure and pain, in contrast with sensations as indifferent perceptions of a certain content.

We do not thereby assert that these two spiritual performances occur separate from each other; we find it much more probable that primarily no mental presentation is completely indifferent, and that rather the value of pleasure or pain attached to it only escapes our attention, because, in educated life the meaning, and the significance, which the impressions have for our purposes in life, has become more important to us than the consideration of the impression itself.

On the other hand, we adhere to the statement that, judged by the very notion of them, sensations and feelings are two different performances which, although always connected, are nevertheless, not deducible from each other. A mere relation of some sort between different simultaneous impressions or states does not, therefore, of itself produce a feeling; this is done only by means of the relation acting as a stimulus on the *entire* nature of the soul, and, since it encites a capacity of the soul of which we have not previously taken account, inducing the soul to a reaction, — namely, to the production of the feeling.

§ 48. It is not demonstrable, but a natural pre-judgment, and a probable hypothesis, that feelings are the results and tokens of the agreement or disagreement between the excitations produced in us, and the conditions of our permanent well-being. Pleasure would therefore depend upon every encitement to the use of our natural capacities within the limits of these conditions, and it would rise in degree with the intensity of these encitements; on the contrary, pain would depend upon the fact that the excitations suffered are at strife with the aforesaid conditions, in part as respects their strength, and in part also, as respects their form (a thing commonly overlooked).

The foregoing statement does not mean that the soul first observes the excitations, and then their relation with respect to these conditions; and finally, according to its view of these acts, decides whether to experience pleasure or pain. The rather, just as sensation — for example, that of red — is merely the result of a series of processes in the nerves, but tells us nothing whatever concerning these processes; so is feeling simply the last result of the aforesaid strife or concord, and it only makes its appearance in consciousness after these unconscious processes.

§ 49. Pleasure and pain are general designations, which, in this form of generality (exactly as, for example, 'color,' too) express nothing actual. The rather has every actual pleasure or pain its own entirely specific character, and it can by no means be made up out of various component parts of a general pleasure and pain; just as the different colors are not produced by different mixtures of bright and dark.

Concerning the conditions, under which the feelings, in general, or definite forms of them, originate, we know almost nothing.

The first group which we are able to distinguish, the *feelings of sense*, — that is to say, those directly dependent on sense-stimuli, — are in the case of the different senses so much the more intensive, the less these senses are capable of fine objective perceptions. Colors and their contrasts merely excite satisfaction or dissatisfaction; dissonances of tones cause suffering to the hearer personally; the pleasure and pain of smell and taste are much more intensive; but it is only in the skin, which of itself alone furnishes little cognition, and in the interior parts, which contribute to cognition nothing whatever, that the pain assumes the character of physical suffering. The purposeful nature of this arrangement is manifest; its mechanical basis is unknown.

§ **50.** These less intense feelings of the higher senses form the transition to a second class, *the æsthetic feelings*, which are not quite exclusively, but in the main, attached to a simultaneous multiplicity of impressions, and in the simplest cases, as a matter of fact, depend on the simplicity or difficulty of the relations which obtain between them. The precise reason, however, on account of which this simplicity — for example, in the case of consonant tones — acts favorably upon us is unknown; for as a rule we do not perceive these relations of fact as such. The character of these æsthetic feelings of satisfaction and dissatisfaction can be expressed, in contrast to sensuous comfort or discomfort, by saying that only the universal spirit in us, and not our merely personal well-being, is furthered or disturbed by these impressions.

In this class are included *the ethical feelings*, of which we are compelled to speak on this account, because moral approbation or disapprobation is nothing else but the expression of a value, or absence of value, which we perceive only in feeling, and which is, on this account, totally distinct from a merely theoretical judgment concerning the truth or untruth of a proposition.

§ 51. A further description of the feelings is useless; it is of use, on the other hand, to distinguish two states thereof.

That is frequently called feeling which is more precisely to be called 'Affection,' and which does not consist in a quiet state or a mere disposition of the mind, but in a movement (as in the case of rage and terror) that also produces disorder in the train of ideas, and besides ordinarily includes unconscious movements, partly mere gestures, and partly the beginnings of actions which would proceed from the inducement given, unless they should be restrained.

In like manner must we distinguish the 'Sentiments,'—that is to say, permanent species of mental constitution, which proceed from this, that a definite value is once for all placed upon certain contents of ideas; they are, therefore,—for example, piety or patriotism,—not themselves simple definite feelings, but causes from which the different species of feelings can originate according to the nature of circumstances.

§ 52. More important still is the connection of feeling with 'Self-consciousness.'

The latter includes two things:—first, that we form some picture or other of us (similar or dissimilar); and, secondly, that we recognize this picture as the picture of *ourselves*.

As far as the first point is concerned, we understand how the picture of our body, because it intrudes into the recollection of all our experiences, appears as the point of issue for our entire spiritual life; and that other experiences likewise incite us to conceive of ourselves as not, to be sure, identical with the body, but as in an obscure manner connected with it. Beyond this point of standing we do not get in ordinary life. It is science which first attempts further to explain (and such, too, will be the task we set ourselves later on) this essential being of the soul itself as well as also the manner of its connection with the body.

On the other hand, we are here met by the second question,—namely: How do we come to hold such a mental picture when attained, not as the picture of some object or other, but as the picture of *our own selves*, and to separate this 'ego' of ours from all the rest of the world by an absolute distinction which has quite another value than the distinction of any other Thing from a second or a third?

It is obvious that the foregoing question cannot be answered by a definition of the general character of '*egohood*';—for example, by the following: The 'Ego' is that subject which is at the same time its own object. For such a general notion corresponds to every 'ego,' and therefore to 'thee' and to 'him' just as well as to 'me.' Self-consciousness, however, ought to set forth, not merely the general spiritual property—which is common to all persons, but it ought to distinguish 'me' from every other person.

And now it may be said: I am the subject of my world of thought, and thou art the subject of thine.

But to say this would be useless, as long as we were not to possess an immediate perspicuity concerning the distinction of what is *mine* from that which is *not* mine.

No merely theoretical consideration can teach the aforesaid distinction. We should be betrayed into an endless circle if we should wish to say, for example: Mine is what I have, and thine is what thou hast.

Nothing else remains, therefore, but to recognize the fact, that that which is *my* state announces itself,—in a manner wholly immediate and admitting of no further deduction,—as something in itself altogether special;—as something, that is to say, which is distinguished from that which is not my state, not merely as this state foreign to me is from a third, but in such manner that we have ample reason for separating this state of our own from all else that occurs in the world, by an incomparable distinction.

Now what is referred to above happens in reality in a very simple way, just by means of feeling. Each of our own states, everything which we ourselves actually suffer, are sensible of, or do, is designated by means of a feeling being immediately attached to it (of pleasure, of pain, of interest, etc.); while this accompaniment is wanting to that which we merely represent mentally as the states, the doing, sensation, suffering, of other beings, but do not ourselves experience or suffer.

Accordingly, no difficult intermediation whatever is necessary, in order to answer the second of the questions proposed above. It amounts only to affirming that a bare *knowing* in general cannot furnish the impulse for this altogether unexampled distinction by means of which every being with a soul sets itself over opposite to all the rest of the world.

§ 53. In the way described above, as we believe, does the meaning of the possessive pronoun 'mine' first become perspicuous. It is not until afterward, when we direct our reflective thought to these circumstances, that we also form the substantive name of the 'ego' as the being to which that belongs which is called 'mine.'

And here a two-fold distinction must be made. The mental picture which we form for ourselves of our own being may be more or less apt or erroneous; that depends upon the elevation of the power of cognition by means of which every being endeavors theoretically to render to itself an explanation concerning this centre of its own mental states. On the other hand, the perspicuity and intimateness with which each being that has feeling distinguishes itself from the entire world does not at all depend on the aptness of this insight of it into its own being, but is expressed in the case of the lowest animals, in so far as they recognize their states as their own by means of physical pain or of pleasure, in just as lively fashion as is the case with the most intelligent spirit. A spirit, however, which should penetrate everything, but have no interest of pleasurable or painful sort in anything, would surely neither be capable of opposing itself as an 'ego' to the rest of the world, nor would it have any inducement so to do. It would only appear to itself as one, but not as one in any way to be preferred, of the many examples of a being which is at the same time subject and object of thought.

And these two achievements, of knowing its own being and of feeling itself as a 'self,' are therefore not necessarily connected with each other. But the first of the two we have to consider as being just that immediate self-feeling, whose presence as well as its liveliness is altogether independent of the degree of the self-cognition which we ordinarily think of, under the name of 'self-consciousness.' The latter is rather nothing more than the interpretation which thought, as it progresses in the further course of our spiritual development, gives to that inner experience which is originally possible only in the form of feeling.

CHAPTER VII.

OF MOTIONS.

§ 54. We execute our bodily movements without knowledge of the means necessary to them, — the muscles and their contractility ; and in particular, without knowing how we must set about to induce thereto a definite motor nerve, that it may throw the muscles necessary for a definite motion into a fitting state of excitation. It follows from this, that in no case does the soul bring the movements about, and execute them in particular, by its own laying hand to it, as it were. The rather does it, without exception, beget nothing more than a certain inner state confined to itself (as of wishing, willing, desiring). With such state, an order of nature, unapproachable to our consciousness and wholly independent of our will, has thereupon connected the originating of a bodily movement as a result in fact. Primarily, therefore, we have nothing to do but to learn to know the different psychical states which are in this manner the occasion of the bodily movements.

§ 55. In a living body changes are ceaselessly happening that also have an influence upon the motor nerves, and occasion motions in the production of which the soul does not participate at all. Nevertheless they are important. For only by means of the fact that motions happen of themselves, and then become objects of its observation, does the soul of an animal arrive at the thought that its body is movable, and that its motions stand in connection with its own inner states; — a thought, at which it would not arrive, if it were dwelling in a body which was never of itself, or by external causes, thrown into motion.

§ 56. Of the before-mentioned motions we may bring forward, as a special class, the *reflex motions.* These are such as originate through the excitation of a sensory nerve by external or internal stimuli being transferred, without the soul's coöperation, in the central organ, to the motor nerves, in such a manner that it arouses to motion with a single shock a group of muscles coördinated for some purposeful action. In this case a conscious sensation may originate at the same time; but the excitation may also, without begetting any such sensation, bend aside, as it were, and produce the same motions without consciousness having any share in them. Many of these motions — like coughing, sneezing, the changes of the pupils of the eye when stimulated by light — admit of being apprehended as reactions which nature has arranged for in the structure of the body as a means of guarding it against injuries. They are shown to be *purely mechanical* results of the excitations, by the fact that they not only proceed involuntarily, but cannot even be inhibited by a mere will to the contrary; for this they rather require some artificial counter-acting agency.

§ **57.** In the *mimetic* and *physiognomic motions* — laughing, weeping, sobbing, and the like — the point of starting in the first instance is a psychical state, — a state, that is, of the mind. As a whole, they do not admit of being counterfeited artificially except in a very imperfect way; even such an imperfect counterfeit is brought about only by artificially transposing one's self through fancy into the same mood of mind as that which is the actual cause of them. All these motions likewise take place without knowledge of their reason and their use; for we cannot tell exactly why we are compelled to laugh at joy and to weep at pain, and not rather the reverse. They are therefore, too, motions which an order of nature, not contrived, and also not understood by us, has attached as results in fact to our states of mind.

§ 58. Another class is composed of the *imitative motions* with which, for example, the observer undesignedly accompanies the thrusts of the fencer or of the player at nine-pins; and with which the uneducated narrator imitates the motions that he describes. In this case it is the mental picture, and of course that of a definite motion, which, without further knowledge and volition, of itself passes over into the execution of the movement.

In this class are to be reckoned the most of our every-day motions, such as we frequently call 'actions.' As soon as, at the end of a series of thoughts, the idea of a motion based upon them emerges in us, and no resistance from any quarter is brought to bear against it, this idea passes over into motion of itself and without our having to assume, or being able to demonstrate, an impulse of the will expressly directed toward the motion. This is true in a very special manner of dexterities previously acquired, — for example, writing, or playing the piano, — where the mere idea of a sound, to be fixed upon or brought forth, immediately induces the necessary motions, without a clear idea of the latter needing to be previously developed in consciousness.

§ 59. The foregoing considerations appear to annul a distinction between *voluntary* and *involuntary motions.* In fact they do not.

Whatever may be our conviction (subsequently to be developed), concerning the nature of the will, we can in no case impute to it the power to do more than to *will.* That an accomplishment of the thing willed follows thereupon, does not depend on *it* at all, but only on the fact that with it, in so far as it is a definite state of the soul different from other states, an order of nature entirely independent of it has connected a definite change, different from other changes, in the state of the motor nerves. Where this is not the case, the will, which is then no more than a futile wish, remains without any results.

An action is therefore 'voluntary' in case the interior initial state, from which a motion would originate as a result, does not merely take place but is approbated or adopted or endorsed by the will. Every action is 'involuntary' which, mechanically considered, issues from the same initial point, and wholly in the same manner, but without having experienced such approbation.

The control of the will over the motions of the body may, accordingly, be compared perhaps to our use of the alphabet. New sounds or letters we are not able to fabricate, but are bound to those which our instruments of speech make possible for us. We can combine them, however, in innumerable ways. And just so the soul, when it combines according to its designs those inner initial states, in whatever series it prefers, can also compound these elements of motions, corporeally made ready as they are beforehand, into the most varied actions for the expression of its will.

Part Second.

THEORETICAL PSYCHOLOGY.

Part Second.

THEORETICAL PSYCHOLOGY.

CHAPTER I.

OF THE SOUL.

§ **60**. After the foregoing complete review of the individual elements of the inner life, we inquire concerning the Nature of the Subject in which they all occur, or are possible. Our final conviction on this point will be made clear in the simplest way if, for the present, we let the current views hold, — such views, that is, as are wont in the first instance to be formed on the inducement of experience; and then gradually transform them, in order to adapt them to the solution of difficulties which they could not solve in their earlier form. It must therefore be considered that everything cannot be said at once, and that only the final form which our view will assume, is our permanent conviction.

§ **61**. The constant connection of the spiritual life with that of the body, in which alone it is the subject of observation, makes the attempt natural to apprehend it, too, as simply the product of the bodily functions.

Nevertheless it is an ancient truth, which has no need whatever of a modern re-discovery, that the origin of a spiritual condition is never analytically comprehensible from all possible combinations of material conditions. Or, more simply said: If we conceive of material elements in such a way that we presuppose nothing in them which does not strictly belong to the conception of *matter;* if we therefore apprehend them merely as space-filling realities, which are movable and can produce motions in each other by means of the forces belonging to them; if, finally, we conceive of these motions, whether of one or of many elements, as no matter how much varied or combined; still the moment never comes when we should be able to say: Now it is self-evident that this motion last produced can no longer remain motion, but must pass over into sensation.

A Materialism, therefore, which should nevertheless assert that the spiritual life could proceed from bare physical states or motions of corporeal atoms, would be a perfectly barren assumption; and in this form, too, materialism has hardly ever been proposed in earnest. The materialistic views which have actually had faith in their own principles, have always taken their point of departure from the other presupposition, — namely, that what they proceed to style 'matter' *is* actually something much better than the name tells, and than what it appears to be from the outside. It is assumed to contain in itself a fundamental property, from which the spiritual states would be able to develop in just the same way as the physical predicates of extension, impenetrability, etc., develop from another fundamental property which it likewise possesses.

Accordingly the new form of the attempt arose; — exactly as physiology deduces the corporeal life from the reciprocal actions of the *physical* forces of all the corporeal elements, exactly so has psychology to explain the spiritual life from the joint action of the *psychical* forces of these elements.

§ **62**. The foregoing view — not inconceivable previous to investigation — nevertheless goes to wreck upon the fact that, it is impossible for it to comprehend the origin of that Unity of Consciousness, which is a fact of experience, and from which we are not at liberty arbitrarily to withdraw our attention, simply because it is very enigmatical, in order then more conveniently to explain the remainder of the content of experience.

It is an error for one to think that it is possible to construe this "unity of consciousness" according to the analogy of the composition of physical forces. For if it is said, that just as a single resultant originates from two different motions, and no further regard is paid to the duality of the causes from which it sprung, so also, can a perfect unity of consciousness proceed from a multiplicity of psychical motions when united;—then this analogy derived from mechanics has been only inaccurately expressed. In truth, the assertion amounts to this: If two motions act upon one and the same indivisible point, or on the same real element, they produce a single resultant, which does not then hover in mid-air, but exists only as a state of the very same simple element on which the components act.

Thus completed, the analogy by no means leads to the result wished for, but directly back to the ordinary view. That is to say, the many elements, even in case they should possess psychical capacity, would produce the unity of consciousness only if there were some one indivisible 'unit-element,' into which all their influences might discharge, as it were, and which by its own nature would be capable of focusing all these impressions in its own consciousness.

§ 63. If we call **a, b . . . z,** the single corporeal elements, each of which may be at the same time physically and psychically endowed, then the question arises, What result, at a given time, can the reciprocal action of each with every other have?

Were they all of like species, and under like conditions, then scarcely anything else could happen but that, at the end of the time, all would be in the same terminal state **Z.** Were this **Z,** therefore, a consciousness, then it would be such, and of course with the same content, repeated as many times over as there are elements which act on each other. On the contrary, a *unity* of consciousness apart from this similarity of all the exemplars of consciousness, would not originate.

In reality, however, the elements **a, b . . . z,** are *not* of like species; but they certainly are subject, in the structure of the organism, to very diverse conditions. Some of them, on account of their inferior nature, and their unfavorable situation, can only receive a few influences from without in an immediate and lively way; others, in themselves superior or more favorably placed, develop a much richer consciousness representing in itself all possible states of the others. Which now of these many dissimilar examples of consciousness is *our own,* — the one we know through inner experience?

We should naturally assume it would be the consciousness of the most preëminent element of all, — the central monad of our body according to Leibnitz. For we find that the changes of our body are most intimately connected with the states of our ego, and that very little happens in it which we should have reason to ascribe to the activity of other centres of consciousness.

§ **64.** According to the foregoing it follows, therefore, that we can in no way get rid of regarding the one and indivisible subject of our consciousness as a party separate by itself; while the other party consists in the body, — that is, in an aggregate or ordered multiplicity of elements which, taken singly, are perhaps kindred to the nature of the soul, and yet are in no case identical with it, but of a different essence.

This assumption — in itself conceivable — of a psychical life in every element of the body, remains otherwise wholly useless for the explanation of *our* soul-life; for if we can never transport ourselves into these states of the elements, they have a value for us merely in so far as they act upon our soul as stimuli, and cause the latter to produce *its own* inner states, which are the only ones known to us. On this account, the material elements also can be further considered merely as being material.

The other assumption, intimately connected with the foregoing, that the soul also on its side has physical properties, perhaps answers to some use; but the ordinary mode of conception has not maintained it, but has set the soul as an immaterial essence, in opposition to the material elements, and has thus at once produced the difficulties of the following chapter.

CHAPTER II.

OF THE RECIPROCAL ACTION BETWEEN SOUL AND BODY.

§ 65. If the possibility of an immaterial essence is conceded (on which point, see later), it is customary to object further, — in that case a reciprocal action between it and the body is at least impossible.

The latter, it is said, would find no point of attachment for its physical forces to the comparatively phantom-like soul; the soul would exercise no motor force by means of its inner states upon the masses of the body; the perfect incomparability of the two therefore abolishes all action between them.

§ 66. To this it is to be replied: We deceive ourselves if we believe we are able in any case to comprehend how it is that a reciprocal action takes place; and if we then regard the relation between body and soul as an *inconvenient exception* in which this effort at explanation does not succeed.

If we observe the motive power of a machine and the way in which its component parts work on each other, we believe we understand its action; because our intuition has in this case attained a view of various things about it. On further reflection, however, we discover that we do not understand the two conditions on which the action of all machines depends, — namely, the cohesion of the solid parts and the communication of motion. We can of course multiply words about the matter: but, in the last result, we are still in ignorance how one part of a solid body manages to hold its neighbor firmly attached to itself; or how it manages to cause a motion, in which it is itself caught, to cease and to reappear in another place. What we therefore actually observe in such cases is merely the external scenery which a series of processes runs through, every single one of which is connected with its successor in a perfectly invisible and incomprehensible manner.

In the relation between body and soul we are not able to follow this series of processes quite so far as we might wish. But if we could follow it, for example, up to the point where the physical excitations act on the soul, this last transition would, of course, be in no respects a matter of intuitive knowledge; but still it would not be in the least degree more incomprehensible than the transition of a motion from one material element to the other.

§ 67. The reason that awakens the doubt to which we alluded is the false assertion — frequently to be met with even in antiquity — that only like things (or what is of like species) can act on each other and be acted on by each other.

One can be tempted to make the foregoing assertion only in case one regards the effect to be produced as a state which is pre-existent ready-made in the efficient cause **a**, and is assumed to be transferred unchanged to **b**, and on this account naturally requires in **b** a lodgement similar to that which it has in **a**, and therefore a comparability in general of **b** with **a**.

In opposition to such a view we derive from metaphysic the conviction, that such a loosing of a state from that of which it is a state, and a transition of it to another subject, is wholly inconceivable. Without any exception the action of an **a** upon a **b** consists in this, that, according to a general order of the world (about which nothing is to be said in this connection) a state α of **a** is for **b** the compelling occasion, on which this **b** produces from its own nature a *new* state β, which as a rule need have no similarity whatever to the state α of **a**; for, as even the most ordinary experience teaches, one and the same influence α has very different results according as the objects **b**, **c**, **d** are different, on which it falls.

We have therefore no justification at all for setting up conditions, which must be fulfilled, if an **a** is to have any effect whatever on a **b**. The likeness or similarity of the two imparts to the possibility of their action no greater comprehensibility or probability; and their unlikeness, or even their perfect incomparability, no less.

§ 68. The demand is frequently made for some *bond* between body and soul, in order to comprehend the possibility of their reciprocal action.

But 'bonds' are needed only to unite those things which do not of themselves act on each other, but are indifferent to each other. The binding power of the bond depends, however, upon this, that its single parts are attached to each other; and this fact we cannot always be explaining over and over by new bonds between; but in the last result it depends upon a perfectly immediate reciprocal action of the single elements which hold each other fast without any conceivable machinery intervening.

We should therefore make use of a bond between body and soul only in case we regarded them as wholly indifferent to each other. But even if we had such a bond, it would be of no service to us; for the definite forms in which the body would accordingly act on the soul, and the soul on it, would by no means proceed from the bare conception of the aforesaid bond, but only from the specific natures of the two elements bound together, and of their obligation to reciprocal action.

Instead, therefore, of *one* such vain bond, we assert that the two are connected by very many peculiarly constituted bonds; each single reciprocal action, to which they are by their natures necessitated, is such a bond, which holds them together, not in a merely general but in a definite way.

§ 69. We proceeded upon the concession that the conception of the soul as an immaterial essence is possible. But now even this is denied. Only things of sense, it is said, are accredited by immediate observation; supersensible matters are invariably products of phantasy.

But only the most elementary view of nature would believe in the sensible properties of colors, taste, hardness, etc., as directly constituting the real being of the 'Thing' apparent. It is now a long time since the conviction gained ground that all these predicates are only phenomena which arise in our consciousness at the excitation of an external somewhat. What, on the other hand, this external reality is, through whose influence these predicates come to be, they do not inform us.

The science of nature therefore very early renounced the pretence of having actual intuitions through the senses of the simplest elements of reality. But in its conception of the atoms, it still for a long time thought of them as formally similar to bodies perceivable by the senses, such as might be supposed to spring from compounding the atoms; that is to say, as being of a very minute and yet of a certain extension, and of an unknown and yet definite shape, and as filling this small volume with a perfect impenetrability.

Manifold difficulties, in which this conception is involved, have also led to the attempt in physics to apprehend the atoms as absolutely without extension or as points that are distinguished from empty points of space merely by their being centres of forces which act outward, as well as real points of seizure, as it were, for forces that come from without. Such a thought has no other meaning than this, that the atoms, too, are in themselves *supersensible* beings:—that is to say, such beings as are not merely in fact, on account of their minuteness, perfectly unapproachable to *our* perception by the senses, but on account of their nature are so to *every* such perception; and that all the intuitions of sense, which at first appear to set before us with exactness what is in itself real, are merely secondary phenomena in which the results of the reciprocal actions of elements, in themselves wholly supersensible, reach our perception.

Accordingly it is not the conception of *immaterial*, but that of *material* being, which is to be scrupled at; and the gap does not exist, which appears to us at first to separate body and soul as two perfectly heterogeneous elements, and to render their reciprocal action impossible.

CHAPTER III.

THE SEAT OF THE SOUL.

§ **70.** An immaterial real being can have no *extension* in space: it may, however, have a position; and this we define as the point up to which all influences from without must be transplanted, in order to make an impression on this being, and from which alone outward this being exercises immediate effects upon its environment. In reference to the soul no one doubts that it is present only within its own body; for it is only here that it acts immediately upon the whole external world, although solely through the mediation of the body.

§ **71.** Now the attempt has been made to conceive of the spatial relation of the soul to the body, in the first place, according to the analogy of our ideas concerning the omnipresence of God.

By this we mean that God is alike near to every point of the world with his immediate activity; that consequently, his will is neither compelled to traverse any way whatever in order to reach an element of the universe **z**; nor does it need any intermediate agency, in order to act on **z**. But we by no means intend by this that the infinite extension of the arena which God thus controls belongs as a spatial property to God himself.

Now in just the same way is the soul assumed to be present everywhere in its body without being itself a space-magnitude.

The foregoing analogy is, however, wholly unserviceable. We have already (to wit, on the occasion of considering the "feelings of double contact") seen, by how complicated means it is that nature succeeds in producing this illusion, so indispensable to the beauty of our life, as though we were present immediately sensitive and moving about in every part of our body. On the contrary, physiological experiments show that the soul stands in immediate reciprocity with absolutely no more than the central organs of the nervous system; and with all the rest of the body only mediately through the nerves themselves.

§ 72. Just as inapplicable is the analogy involved in a second way of representation, to which natural science accustoms us; to wit, that of a physical force which acts immediately, and without any intervening mechanism, in all infinitely remote regions, but with a graded intensity, that is, one that diminishes with the distance. On account of the first circumstance we should be able to say of that body which is the conveyer of the force, — It is in space everywhere; on account of the second, we still ascribe to it a limited situation in space, namely, there where its action is greatest.

But the smallest interruption in the continuity of a nerve, even in the closest proximity to the brain, abolishes the reciprocal action of the soul with that region of the body over which the same nerve is expanded. It has therefore no power which acts at a distance, such as would be able to stretch itself over and beyond this interruption.

Nothing remains for us then but the third analogy, namely, that of effects which follow upon contact by communication of motions.

§ 73. The last analogy has been chiefly followed, and search has been made for such a point in the central organs, in which all the sensory nerves unite, in order there to render their messages, and from which all the motor nerves issue forth, in order to conduct the excitations there received over to the body.

The above-mentioned idea not only has certain inner difficulties, but is essentially out of accord with our empirical cognition. Not merely is it true that no such terminal point for the entire net-work of nerves has hitherto been discovered; but there is even the most well-founded cause for the assertion that it never will be found.

The question now arises, how we can ever still maintain under these circumstances the conception of a seat for the soul.

§ **74.** We recur to our original definition of such a seat, but we interpret it still further by the following means.

We are in error if we say that a being is first in a place, and then in consequence thereof is able to act on its environment. As long as we continue to abstract from the effects, it can by no means be made clear, precisely in what the Thing's being at this place consists; and whereby this is distinguished from its being at another place, at which the Thing would exist exactly as well as at the former place. We believe rather that the order of the thoughts must be reversed, and we must say: If it is involved in the nature of a being **a**, in general to interchange actions and reactions with **b**, **c**, **d**, then its systematic position in the coherency of things is determined thereby, and in the spatial arrangement of the world it is that point whose immediate environment is constituted by **b**, **c**, and **d**.

Now in general, the connection of all things may

be so many-sided that an element **a** is not merely destined to enter into reciprocal action with the group **b**, **c**, **d**, but also just as immediately with another group **p**, **q**, **r**; while, nevertheless, **p**, **q**, **r** on account of other different relations do not possess their systematic position with **b**, **c**, **d**, and therefore do not have their spatial position in the neighborhood of the latter, but separated by a distance from them. In this case the active element **a** will have not *one* but, with equal right, *several* special positions without on this account itself falling into a multitude of pieces; precisely as we should think of God as present everywhere and still not in Himself extended. Omnipresence would, of course, comprehend all space: in this case, on the contrary, we should be compelled to require in particular that several positions separated in space should be ascribed to the immaterial being; and that these positions should be separated from each other by intervening spaces in which its presence would not be found in the same way. But no special difficulty is involved in this. We have merely to overcome the customary propensity of our power of imagination, which might persist in apprehending the immaterial being after the model of a corporeal atom, and in ascribing to it, on this account, a visible circumscribed magnitude and form, and accordingly also only *one* position in space.

§ 75. The question still remains unanswered, Why then should single parts of the brain have the preference of being 'seats' of the soul, and other parts, on the contrary, not be thus preferred; although still, so far as we know, there exist no significant differences in their structure or composition?

On this point, too, we are compelled to alter a customary representation. An element **a** is not destined to stand at all times in reciprocal relations with a certain other sort of element **b**, and not with a third sort **c**; the rather is every being **a** interested, or excited to action, only through what happens in other beings. If this **X**, on occurring, is, according to the plan of the whole arrangement of the world, the conditioning premise from which the new state is to originate in **a**, then it, too, *does* originate; and in such case **a** experiences the influence of this **X**, whether this came about in **b** or in **c**. If, on the contrary, **X** is not such premise, then **a** remains in equilibrium and unaltered, whether now **X** takes place in a **b** or in a **c**.

Now just so will the soul enter into reciprocal action only with those points of the central organs in which all the combinations, equilibrations, and elaborations of the physical excitations are executed; and only after the perfecting of the former do the latter, it is assumed, reach the soul's cognition or become legitimate encitements of its activity.

§ **76.** If therefore any one should be able to observe with a microscope what goes on in the interior of the brain, just as accurately as the anatomical structure admits of being observed, superficially everything would appear precisely as materialism asserts. That is to say, at different points of the brain individual psychical processes would be set up on occasion of the physical processes taking their course thither; and nowhere would a being of the soul in its unity show itself as the object of such contemplation.

But the *interpretation*, which materialism gives of this matter of fact, we do not share. These psychical functions do not originate from those physical processes as an addendum, or a product, that carries its own explanation with it: they are invariably possible only in case we apprehend these latter as mere stimuli which act upon the peculiar nature of the soul's essential being, — everywhere present here and not bound to one seat of the form of a mathematical point, — and which cause it to exercise its own capacities.

CHAPTER IV.

THE TIME-RELATIONS OF THE SOUL.

§ **77.** Mere experience could only lead us to the thought:—The soul originates with the body, and with it perishes as well. Necessities of quite another order, which are foreign to this theoretical investigation, have excited the wish to make sure of its immortality; and the attempt has been made to do this by subordinating it under a conception of 'Substance,' which would *per se* contain the predicate of indestructibility.

Such subordination leads, in the first place, to two inconvenient consequences, which one would gladly avoid. That is to say, the reasons on account of which the *human* soul might be subordinated under this conception of substance would also hold good for every animal soul. On the other hand, indestructibility would include, not merely immortality after death, but also unending pre-existence before the present life; and with the latter we neither know how to make a beginning, nor do we find in our experience any evidence for such a previous life.

Finally, moreover, the question would be asked:

Whether, in case the conception of substance includes such an impossibility of ceasing to be, it is of any use whatever, and not a mere figment of the brain; and whether, in the former case, the soul certainly belongs to what must be included under the conception.

§ 78. Now 'Substance' is in fact nothing but a *title* which is attached to everything that has the power to act on something else, and be acted upon by something else, to experience different states, and in the interchange of such states to do work as a permanent unity.

On the contrary, it is a figment of the brain to believe we can discover yet further explanations on the point, how the capacity for such mode of behavior is brought to pass; and to seek for such explanation in thinking of a bit of rigid and indestructible substance as being included in everything, and of all the rest of the properties or states, by which one such thing is distinguished from another, as being grouped about this firm kernel. If one attempts actually to make use of such a conception, it uniformly shows itself completely useless in explaining the phenomena for the sake of which it was assumed. It does not admit of being shown how such a substantial kernel could consist with the manifoldness and changeableness of the properties of which it is asserted (and this, too, again with a word devoid of meaning) that they 'inhere' in it.

Briefly expressed, then: Things are not 'things' by means of a so-called *substance* being concealed in them; but, because they are such as they are, and behave themselves in the manner in which they do behave themselves, they produce for our imagination the false appearance, as though such a substance existed in them as the basis of their behavior.

Now the soul, so long as it does not merely exhibit itself to others as a "unit-subject" of its interior states, but is itself conscious thereof, deserves in the fullest measure this title of a "substance" or real being.

On the other hand, nothing whatever justifies us in making the assertion that just this capacity, if it is once exercised, must then eternally be exercised, and cannot in the course of things be originated or perish again.

§ **79.** To reach a decision on this point, we borrow from Metaphysic a conviction that stands in opposition to the ideas to which the investigation of nature has accustomed us.

For the latter believes that the course of the world admits of being explained by the assumption of a multiplicity of original elements, which are held to be independent of each other in such manner that each could exist alone even if all the others were not; which, further, have in themselves no necessary relation to one another, but in fact have either been subsequently drawn into such relations or have stood in them even from eternity; and which, finally, are compelled by general laws to exercise this reciprocal action in this relation, and another action in a different relation.

On the contrary, we affirm briefly this: No influence whatever of one element on another is really conceivable without self-contradiction, as long as these elements are thought of as originally independent of each other and devoid of relation toward each other. Such influence is only possible in case we consider them all simply as modifications, dependent and constantly related to each other, of One single truly existent Being, which is in them all as the ground of their existence; — the ground, further, on account of which they are compelled to effectuate somewhat definite under fixed conditions, and the ground, finally, of this also, that these prescribed obligations are able to attain to accomplishment.

Or, to express the same truth in another way, all 'Things' are what they are, and accomplish what they do accomplish, not by means of a natural right which became theirs previous to the existence of the world, so that subsequently the world was compelled to govern itself accordingly, and could only actualize that which these privileged ones allowed. The rather is it true that Things are and accomplish all, only on the commission, as it were, of this One true Being; and all which we commonly regard as ultimate unchangeable elements and laws of the world's course, has this unchangeableness and this value, too, only on commission of the plan for the actualization of which it is bound to serve.

§ 80. The foregoing way of apprehending the matter has not been devised, for the first time, in favor of our present inquiry. It is rather necessary, in order to comprehend even the most insignificant action of one element on another. But it admits of an application to the case we are now considering.

It may even be a part of the plan of actuality, that over a wide domain all its changing phenomena are effectuated by means of combinations of unalterable elements and according to the rule of universal laws. Accordingly, there exist in the world these constant masses, the activity of which always results in like manner, and which are nothing else but "*actions*" uniformly maintained or exercised by the aforesaid sole Existence.

But in the same way it may be a part of the before-mentioned plan, that other elements make their appearance only at definite points of time in the world's course, — that is to say, when all the preliminary conditions are actualized, which, according to the plan of the whole, may form the basis of their existence. But nothing hinders these elements, too, in case they have originated, from maintaining themselves as real units, indivisible and independent centres of ingoing and outgoing effects.

Among *such* elements do we reckon the Soul. But a further inquiry, as to how this its independence is brought about, we dismiss as quite out of place. We should just as little be able to specify how it is reached, or brought about, that one of those constant elemental masses can exist and maintain itself forever.

§ **81.** At the place where, and at the moment when, the germ of an organic being is formed amid the coherent system of the physical course of nature, this fact furnishes the encitement or the moving reason, which induces that all-comprehending One Being, — present not otherwheres, but even here, — to beget from himself, besides, as a consistent supplement to such physical fact, the soul belonging to this organism.

Superficially regarded, therefore, Materialism has the right of it here also; that is to say, the soul also originates *in* and *with* the body, but, in sooth, not *of* and *through* it. And all inquiries are useless concerning the manner in which it is, as it were, joined from the outside with the body.

Touching *Immortality*, on the other hand, it is no subject for theoretical decision. In general we simply hold the principle to be valid, that everything which has once originated will endure forever, as soon as it possesses an unalterable value for the coherent system of the world; but it will, as a matter of course, in turn cease to be, if this is not the case. However, this principle is wholly inapplicable in our human hands; we cannot presume to tell in what the merits might consist which justify such duration; or in what the deficiency which makes it impossible.

CHAPTER V.

THE SOUL'S ESSENCE.

§ 82. In investigating the 'Essence' of a Thing we may wish to know, in the first place: whereby *this* thing is distinguished from others; and second: how it is possible for the content thus designated to exist as *real Thing*.

The second inquiry admits of being answered in the case of objects whose distinguishing character consists simply in the shaping of a previously existing material; we are then wont to consider just this material as the *essence* and the aforesaid *form* as only unessential. But a simple material itself, like every simple essence, can never consist of somewhat other than it is itself.

On the other hand, to specify how it is brought about that any so-called 'content' whatever can be, act, and be acted upon, as a 'Thing,' we have already often declined to consider, as an unanswerable inquiry. Accordingly, our discourse can only be of this: by what peculiar character, which constitutes its essence, the soul is distinguished from other substances.

§ 83. We have no other way of learning what is the nature of any Thing, even that of matter, except by its achievements and its effects. It is therefore no fault of psychology, but the most natural way of procedure, to determine in this manner, by reasoning backward, the nature of the soul.

The first systematic attempt at this, the doctrine of the soul's faculties, has certainly remained without result. The various psychical achievements were classified according to their similarity; and it was then of course correct to assume, besides, a 'faculty' for every such group of actual achievements. But this conception was not so fruitful as that of 'force' for the science of physics. For the physicist does not speak of force seriously until the time when he is able to specify, not merely a form of action, but also a law according to which the magnitude of the action alters in proportion to the alteration of certain conditions.

The faculties of the soul, on the contrary, were merely abstracted from the form of the achievements themselves, and no law for them was known; it amounted, accordingly, merely to the tautology that, for example, the faculty of sensation produces sensations; but nothing was known as to what sensations under what conditions.

On the other hand, physics is only so far perfected as it is possible to reduce all natural processes to mere motions of masses. By means of such specific likeness in what happens, it is possible accurately to determine the result which originates from the simultaneous co-operation of different forces upon the same object. On the contrary, the psychical states could be reduced to no such common measure. What must originate, therefore, in case an act of the faculty of feeling coincides with an act of the faculty of representation, does not admit in the least of being conjectured on grounds of this theory. What is known on that point is known independently of the theory,—on grounds of experience and knowledge of men.

Neither of these two deficiencies is to be set aside by any improved carrying out of this theory. It can therefore hold good simply as a summary catalogueing of spiritual achievements, but not as an explanation.

§ 84. The unproductiveness of the above-mentioned theory, and the slight account that it took of the connection of the different faculties, which it nevertheless always regarded as expressions of a soul that is a unity in the strictest sense, induced Herbart to attempt to demonstrate all spiritual activities and all these faculties as a series of results that spring successively from a single primitive activity of the soul.

The soul, he held, is one of those supersensible real beings of perfectly simple quality, which left to themselves alone would always remain unmoved the same, but which, on the other hand, would exercise activities of 'self-preservation' as soon as they are exposed to external stimuli whose influence, if it took effect, would cause a disturbance of their nature. And indeed these acts of self-preservation are different in kind, according as the disturbances through which they are induced are different. Of the rest of real things, — for example, those which lie at the basis of matter, — we are not able to know precisely in what their self-preservation consists. Of the soul, on the contrary, we do know, or believe that we are bound to assume, that they are universally in the form of the *idea*. By means of physical stimuli, whose influence Herbart did not follow further, these inducements to self-preservation are imparted to the soul, and the ideas here originating — that is, simple sensations, of a definite color, of a tone, of a taste — are now the simple elements out of whose further reciprocal action the totality of the rest of the soul's life is assumed to originate.

We here simply refer with gratitude to the explanations previously alluded to, which the course of ideas has received, in accordance with general mechanical laws, by means of the above-mentioned view. On the other hand, we cannot accord with the attempt to derive all the soul's higher activities as self-evident mechanical products of this course of ideas without presupposing any one of those faculties that have not as yet attained to an expression of themselves. This principle was not at all necessary, for Herbart himself confessed that even the simple sensations divide up into quite different classes, — colors, tones, tastes, etc., — no one of which is deducible from the others; that the soul, therefore, really possesses quite distinct faculties which we are not able really to deduce from its unity, although we certainly hold fast by such unity. Nothing therefore would have hindered the assumption that these simple sensations also and their relations to each other acted as new stimuli upon the whole soul, and then called forth in it wholly new reactions which could by no means be derived from the aforesaid inducements alone.

Such an assumption as the foregoing could be refuted only by the demonstration that it is unnecessary, and that in reality all higher spiritual activities are perfectly self-evident consequences of the mutual impact, as it were, of the simple ideas. Such demonstration has not succeeded; — on which point reference may be made to the following examples.

§ 85. We have already in previous articles found it to be impossible that a soul, were it simply an ideating being, should apprehend the relations between its ideas otherwise than they are, and therefore as spatial while they are really non-spatial. If it nevertheless does so, then it manifestly adds out of its own nature to this matter of fact something new which does not follow of itself.

Just as impossible was it to regard attention as mere intensity of the idea itself; for then the subject would be wanting, which exercises all those relating activities in which every actual work of attention consists.

Just now we found it quite as impossible to consider feelings of pleasure or pain as self-evident results of the different situations in which the ideas can come to be toward each other during their course. Were the soul simply an 'ideating being' then it would only ideate all these facts, even if they contained its own destruction, with accuracy and complete indifference. That it takes an *interest* therein, is a new fact which must flow from another peculiarity of its essential being.

Finally, no one will be persuaded that what we mean when we say, "I will," has no other significance than the arising in consciousness of an idea, in a struggle with forces which seek to hinder it. However obscure and mysterious the other thing which we mean by that expression may be, — namely, that in this case not a mere *occurrence* but a *deed* is before us, which is accomplished by ourselves as the one subject of our entire world of ideas; still the fact itself, which we do thus designate and discover in immediate inner experience, cannot be got out of the way by this hypothesis, utterly failing as it does, to explain how even the simple appearance of such acting (in contrast with mere happening) can originate in our view.

We accordingly conclude with the following conviction: It was possible and necessary to entrust to the soul as a unity much more than the bare capacity for having ideas; and even those acts of self-preservation of the primary order, which arose as 'ideas' in consequence of external stimuli, could subsequently by means of their relations and combinations come to be new internal stimuli by which the other capacities of the soul, not previously taken into account, were induced to express themselves.

§ 86. We should therefore be compelled to surrender the attempt to comprehend the origin of the higher spiritual activities from the lower. Instead of such a mechanical construction, however, another way of apprehending the matter admits of being substituted, — a way which would show that, in any case, the collective whole of spiritual expressions — let them originate as they will — fit into one another, and are collectively necessary in order perfectly to actualize the *Idea* which expresses the soul's destiny. Such an attempt did the idealistic systems make; and, last, that of Hegel.

The world in general, they held, is no mere fact, but has also a meaning. In this totality every individual has its definite place; and the essence of each Thing consists, strictly speaking, only in the partial idea whose actualization is committed to it, and by means of which it makes its own contribution to the uninterrupted fulfilment of the highest or total Idea of the world. Could we now formulate for this highest Idea an accurate and exhaustive expression, then we should be able to deduce from it the shape of each Thing, the collective whole of the capacities necessary to it, and, finally, the general laws according to which these must act in order to attain the aforesaid destiny.

But since the foregoing presupposition does not

admit of fulfilment, instead of a scientific deduction that is accessible to proof and counter-proof, only such an one can be secured as, with more or less of taste, greater or less of æsthetic justification, places the individual spiritual activities in connection with a more or less profoundly apprehended expression which is thought to have been discovered for the aforesaid highest Idea.

The ingenious conceptions, which are after all still possible, and which have not been wanting, have moreover been rendered one-sided by an historical circumstance. The inquiry into the kind and truth of our cognition, or into the relation between subject and object, had so much riveted all attention, that the process by which the Existent attains to the apprehension of itself — that is to say, the development of self-consciousness — was held to be the genuine goal or ultimate content of the entire ordering of the world. And now the soul, too, appeared destined to solve this problem of 'self-mirroring' within the bounds of the earthly life; and the different forms in which this problem of pure intelligence is progressively more and more completely solved, occupied pretty nearly the whole space in psychology. But the content of that which is known by sense, intuited, or conceived, withdrew on the other hand, as much into the background, as all the rest of the soul's life, — the feelings and efforts; and the latter themselves came again into consideration only in so far as they also could be put into relation with the aforesaid formal problem of self-objectifying.

CHAPTER VI.

THE CHANGEABLE STATES OF THE SOUL.

§ 87. The life of the soul does not consist in the uniform possession but in the changeable exercise of its capacities. In this regard we find it in manifest dependence on the body; but for the most part attain the possibility of more accurately defining this dependence only on occasion of definite disturbances of the body.

The observations which may be made on this subject admit, however, of three interpretations. In the first place, it might be that an organ now destroyed has been the productive cause of the spiritual function which becomes impossible after the destruction of the organ. It might be in the second place, that this organ has been the exclusive medium of those stimuli of which the soul has need, in order that it may be induced to the exercise of a function that is otherwise comprehensible only from the soul's own nature. Lastly, and in the third place, it might be that the destruction of the organ, either immediately or by virtue of the alteration by which it is followed in other organs, exercises upon the soul a positive effect, although of an *inhibitory* kind; and thereby prevents for a time the expression of a capacity which, in itself considered, continues to exist.

Only the first of these interpretations appears to us in itself untenable, on account of the impossibility of comprehending psychical functions as self-evident products of physical processes. But if we desired to know how both are to be understood simply as united in fact, then one of the two other interpretations besides would be necessary in each individual case. Only the latter, therefore, need be tested further.

§ 88. If by *Consciousness* we understand what we yet more clearly call our 'waking state,' then the question arises, first: Upon what does its opposite, namely, unconsciousness, depend, — the primary example of which is normal sleep.

Now in relation to this it is perfectly manifest that, in general, both the above-mentioned modes of explanation are admissible; but that, still the occurrence of sleep (which in the case of healthy persons results very quickly, and after having found them only a moment since in the full possession of their spiritual powers), and the possibility of its interruption, does not argue an exhaustion of the nervous forces, which would now be unable longer to supply the stimuli necessary for the maintenance of the waking condition, but rather a positive inhibition consisting in all manner of minute feelings of weariness, that, in the aggregate, diminish the interest of the soul in the carrying-on of the life of thought, and that have attained a heightened effectiveness just on account of this surrender of the soul to them.

Sudden unconsciousness from fright appears to originate in like manner. Considered as a mere physical stimulus, the frightful sight or report is very insignificant and harmless. It is only our reflection, which interprets the significance thereof in its total connection with our life, that gives to what is perceived this power to frighten us. From this point on, the course of our spiritual functions may immediately be disturbed, and the bodily powerlessness which follows thereupon may simply be the reaction of the psychical disturbances.

Even unconsciousness in sickness, or after injuries of the brain, does not wholly exclude this view of the subject. The inhibitory influences are partially observable in the form of pain; this is not, however, necessary. Just as we observe nothing whatever of the states prevailing in our nerves previous to sensation, but only the latter itself appears in consciousness, so may consciousness also vanish without the work of the forces which inhibited it needing previously to become an object of perception.

§ 89. Manifold thought has been bestowed in recent times upon the effectiveness of certain stimuli in maintaining the state of waking, or of their absence in producing unconsciousness.

From experiments in hypnotism it has been concluded that, by the complete exclusion of external sense-stimuli, and by the prevention of motion, the whole spiritual movement becomes so depressed that the waking state cannot be maintained, but complete unconsciousness takes place, — a process which in a few cases has been observed even in human beings, but which affords no trustworthy conclusions.

As for the rest, we know that if our inner movement of thought, which is maintained by some interest or other, does not take place, — therefore, in states of ennui, — even the influence of external stimuli that do still actually take place, does not prevent our falling asleep.

Positive influences too are known, which dispose us to falling asleep; such as a number of regularly recurring rhythmic movements of the body, rocking, stroking, combing the head, constant looking at large illuminated uniform surfaces, the convergence of the axes of the eyes in squinting, etc. Finally, the manipulations of the mesmerist belong under this head. But all these methods are not a fit basis for critical judgment, on account of the fact that the instances of their inefficacy are extraordinarily frequent, and they consequently admit of the assumption of some adjunct condition of their result as yet unknown.

But in all cases, at the very most, only the external means on the one hand, and its effect on the other hand, are known to us; the intermediate processes which connect the former with the latter are quite obscure.

§ 90. If the minimum of the waking state — that is, the sensation of external impressions — be present, it is not necessary on this account that the next higher activity, — that is, the consciousness of the *relations* between the single impressions, — should also be connected therewith. It is well known that, in our quite ordinary experience, this latter action is often wanting; for example, in cases when the impressions are foreign to a train of thought which we are attentively following, or in cases when our mind is moved with painful emotions. Moreover, there are also pathological disturbances, of a nature indeed as yet unknown, which form the conditions (§ 25) of this incapacity (recently called 'soul-blindness') for reflective combination or for the understanding of impressions perceived by the senses.

§ **91.** The unconsciousness of sleep is in general of varied *depth*, which admits of being measured by the magnitude of the excitations that are necessary for waking. It is, however, very frequently imperfect in so far as, for example, excitements of the sense of hearing and of touch still act on the consciousness and occasion the corresponding sensations.

Nevertheless, since in sleep there is an absence of the attention guided by design, which, during waking hours and principally by the help of the sense of sight, is conscious of the entire connection of the surrounding reality, those sensations now reproduce, without any selection of what is probable, such others as they cohere with in respect to their bare content, or as have been brought into coherency by means of some earlier train of ideas.

Accordingly, that phantastic character dreams have is set agoing, which very frequently gather close around some small nucleus of an actual sensation details of scenery that, although in accord with it, have no connection at all with the reality.

Such activity of consciousness in sleep admits of being heightened so that questions may be answered correctly; and it is, therefore, so far forth made possible for the spirit of one who is awake to direct to some extent the course of the dreamer's thought, and perhaps even his actions. For in such a case no collective consciousness of actual surroundings, and of one's personal situation in them, stands in the way of the immediate transition of the idea of an action, when once aroused, into actual accomplishment.

§ **92.** For the retention of ideas once acquired and therefore for the fact of *Memory*, we should not suppose that a corporeal basis is needed; since even in the case of material elements we are unable to demonstrate how far it is exactly their materiality which is the basis of the observed persistence of their states. On this account we might as well ascribe this property to every immaterial subject which is at all capable of acting and being acted upon.

But the necessity for thinking of innumerable different impressions as enduring unmixed in the perfect unity of the soul would favor the other thought, that this problem could be much better satisfied by a great multiplicity of elements. We should not think of it as though the impressions left behind them a state of *quiescence* as an after-effect. We should rather follow the analogy of the vibrations of light and sound, and conceive of *motions* which extend over many elements and, in spite of single disturbances, are further transplanted after their intersection. Only it would be impossible to make this general analogy of any value in detail. Each image of an approaching object would at every instant be the source for new vibrations which are not covered by the preceding ones. How one idea of the object is to originate from these; again, how two simultaneous motions are to be associated with one another in such manner that the renewal of the one sets the other agoing again, without resulting in a special new impact for the latter; finally, how it comes about that a motion which belongs to a partial impression of a composite image re-awakens exactly those others which belong with it as other parts of the same image;—for the answer to all these questions there is a complete lack of physical analogies.

If, accordingly, a corporeal basis of memory appears unnecessary, still pathological observations show that such a basis nevertheless exists in some manner or other. The fact that those events which immediately precede an attack of illness easily remain forgotten may be put upon the ground that their mental picture has been associated with a general feeling of illness, which no longer exists after recovery, so that such recollections want the lever that could reproduce them. But other facts, such as the incapacity for recalling certain groups of ideas that are substantially similar — for example, surnames or single parts of speech — have hitherto been inaccessible to explanation.

§ 93. We ascribe considerable influence over the course of all the spiritual states to the *Temperaments;* — by which we understand nothing more than the differences, in kind and degree, of excitability for external impressions; the greater or less extent to which the ideas excited reproduce others; the rapidity with which the ideas vary; the strength with which feelings of pleasure and pain are associated with them; finally, the ease with which external actions associate with these inner states themselves.

Immeasurably different as the temperaments, in this meaning of the word, are, nevertheless the four well-known ones may be mentioned as the most definite types: the sanguine with its great rapidity of change and lively excitability; the phlegmatic, with slightly varied and slow, but not on this account, weak reactions; the choleric, with one-sided receptivity and great energy in single directions; instead of the melancholic and preferably, the sentimental, — distinguished by special receptivity for the feeling of the value of all possible relations, but indifferent toward bare matter of fact.

One must guard one's self against confusing the temperaments with various pathological conditions or peculiarities of character; although it is perfectly obvious that each has its own peculiar strong and weak sides, for moral culture and bodily health. Concerning the corporeal basis of temperaments we know nothing decisive.

§ 94. Phrenology or cranioscopy has believed that it could demonstrate a series of organs for the individual spiritual functions. Its belief is, indeed, without any foundation in so far as it separated these organs in space and sought to define their position; on the contrary, it was certainly not entirely baseless, when it regarded certain external formations — for example, of the skull — merely as indications which betray and guarantee the fact that conditions, otherwise wholly unknown, exist, on which depend the realization or the special particular intensity of the aforesaid functions, in a manner not further demonstrable but given as matter of fact.

It was moreover prevented from making such a useful collection of facts, by another fault. Only those functions or talents could profitably be taken into account, the meaning of which is unambiguous, and which can neither well be concealed when present, nor counterfeited when absent — for example, musical, artistic, mathematical talents; of all of which we have examples enough as inherited within a family. On the contrary, characteristics which can only be estimated by a refined knowledge of men, and even then never with certainty, and which in a given case may be the product not merely of natural disposition but of education and of accident, are not at all adapted for being determined in this way, although they have been most frequently so employed.

§ 95. A *sensorium commune*, and in more recent times, a *motorium commune* have been distinguished.

A necessary function for the first of the two might perhaps be found in this, that the individual impressions do not as such become an object for the soul's cognition, but only after combinations or other adjustments have taken place. This work of elaboration the organ would have to accomplish; a mere collecting of the impressions in one place would seem superfluous. Now how far such a process extends we do not know; apparently it accords with what was previously said in reference to our space-intuitions, — to which perhaps a greater part of the brain is appropriated.

It would be required of the *motorium commune* that it should combine the individual motor nerve-roots with each other in such various ways that a series of subordinated centres originates, each of which needs only a *single* excitation in order simultaneously to set agoing several motions that are combined in a purposeful way. But the nature of the influence which the soul itself exercises upon these points is certainly incorrectly represented, if we conceive of impulses as proceeding from the soul, that are of the same species and distinguished in their effects merely by the direction which they take, and hence by the different terminal points which they reach. To determine such a direction would be impossible for the soul without a knowledge of the structure of the brain, with which we cannot credit it. We therefore assert, on the contrary, that every idea of a motion **a**, which originates in the soul, is a qualitatively different state from the other idea of a motion **b**. To **a**, accordingly, belongs a resulting state α, to **b** another, β. These two states could only originate in those points of the nervous mass, which by their organization are exactly capable of being stimulated to produce them; just as a glass, for example, resounds only to those tones which, on its being struck, it would produce by virtue of its own tension. The impulses of the soul do not therefore need to be *directed*, but spontaneously find the places where they are effective; naturally, when the case is rightly understood, in such a way that they do not have to traverse a certain distance from a given point to that place.

In similar manner should we conceive of the function of the organ of speech — the only one which has thus far been discovered with any great certainty at a definite spot in the hemispheres of the large brain. Extirpation of this spot destroys the capacity for combining the representative 'sound-pictures' of a word with the excitement of the motions in the muscles of speech, as would be required for the actual utterance of the word. Although we can in this case form but little conception of the kind of action which constitutes the function of this organ, we are yet more in the dark as to how such a disturbance of its action can be brought about as is presented to us in the type of disease called 'aphasia.'

§ **96.** For all the higher spiritual capacities, which consist in judgment of the relations of given conceptions, we neither know how empirically to demonstrate a definite bodily organ, nor should we know how to conceive precisely what, that is of any use, such an organ could contribute toward the solution of the most essential part of this problem — that is, the pronouncing of the judgment itself. It is conceivable, on the other hand, that these higher activities might presuppose the complete and clear representation of the content about which the judgment is to be passed; and, consequently, also the undisturbed function of those organs which contribute first to perception by the senses, then to its reproduction and combination with other perceptions, and, finally, to the appropriate attachment of feelings of value to each of them.

§ 97. There remains a large number of narratives concerning extraordinary spiritual activity in states of bodily ailment. The various points thereof are not all alike unworthy of belief.

The assertion that there are cases of an immediate (without the agency of any physical medium) '*rapport*' between consciousness and distant parts of the external world, does not admit of refutation *a priori;* for all effects through media must, in the last analysis, be based upon immediate effects. Only experience can teach us where such effects are met with, and where not; and it certainly does teach us that the entire spiritual life, awake and healthy, and so accessible to safe experiment, is universally connected with the external world only through physical media.

On the other hand, the assumption is at all events senseless, that the precise phenomena which are supposed to be perceived can be explained in the lump by the efflux and influx of an animal magnetism.

Again, it is not impossible that the same simple sensation — for example, that of light — may also originate in other nerves which are not specifically designed for it; on the contrary, it is quite impossible that an orderly apprehension of a multiplicity of sensations — for example, the reading of a letter — should result through the nerves of the skin, which are not (like the optic nerve) constructed for such a combination of impressions.

It is possible, finally, that all manner of spiritual functions take place with more liveliness in such pathological conditions as diminish the regular intercourse with the external world, and thereby remove all the minute circumspection and timorousness which in ordinary life oppose the exercise of a given capacity. In such cases — for example, when problems previously insoluble are solved in somnambulance — this achievement is never accomplished except with the help of the capacities which have been gained in waking life.

Finally, that in such states nothing higher is attained than would be attainable to ordinary human nature, is shown by the insignificant content of all the revelations alleged to be received in them; as well as by the fact that the many examples of such cases in history have never been allied with any advance in our knowledge.

CHAPTER VII.

THE REALM OF SOULS.

§ 98. The requirement that we should speak of a 'soul' is of course first made upon us at the point where facts would be incomprehensible without this assumption. In reality, however, the endowing of things with a soul may extend further than this requirement.

In fact all Things have been spoken of as though endowed with souls; but this thought, for which we may have good grounds, has thus far been unfruitful for the explanation of individual phenomena. With still greater predilection have 'plant-souls' been spoken of (Fechner, "Nanna or the soul-life of plants." Leipzig, 1848). And certainly the possession of a soul is by no means bound to the centralized structure which we observe in the animal and find wanting in the plant. Nevertheless, the more the organization of the plant and consequently also the expressions by means of which it might make intelligible to us whatever inner life it happens to have, vary from such structure, so much the less is it possible to construct from this fancy, however correct, an object of science.

The animal kingdom alone remains, therefore, as affording us an ascending series of spiritual life.

§ 99. It would be an error to regard all animal souls as beings of originally the same sort, which were merely afterwards either equipped with more or fewer faculties, or else adapted for their greater or less elevation and for the peculiarities of their spiritual culture, by the variety of the external impressions made upon them. As before, so now we consider the word 'Soul' simply as a title which belongs to all beings that have an experience of their own inner states and reactions upon stimuli, in the form of ideas, feelings, and acts of will. But what is expressed in this common term — that is, the peculiar essence of the soul — may be as radically different as we conceive gold, silver, and lead originally to be, although they all have the power of expressing themselves only by differences in degree of the same physical transactions, — gravity, cohesion, hardness, etc.

The question may arise as to where we begin to deal with the *Instinct* of animals; under which is to be reckoned not merely certain wonderful artistic impulses, but, properly speaking, the entire typical mode of life of each species of animals. Perhaps, especially in the lower classes of animals, the souls are by no means destined, to the same extent as human souls, for learning from experience; but, in accordance with their bodily organization, have an original content of consciousness, by which they are controlled just as we sometimes are by an idea that has arisen perchance in a dream. But this assumption cannot be turned to further profit. As an additional aid in explanation it is to be said further, that, in case of a wholly different structure of the nervous system, the vegetative processes, of which we remain entirely unconscious, are in the lower animals permanent objects of perception and points of starting for acts which appear to us groundless. And not less may there be sensations of external circumstances for which we lack the requisite organs, — for example, sensations of minute electrical changes in the environment, from which the sensitiveness to changes of weather results not as foresight of the future but as perception of what has already occurred.

It would, nevertheless, be incorrect to limit all the soul-life of animals to such 'instinct'; the rather does an accommodation to the circumstances take place in their actions, so that obviously the same interpretation and use of experience as that on which our every-day life is based, must have taken place in their case also.

§ 100. If the *Intellect* and its function — namely, thinking — be considered as characteristic of man, what we mean by this is, that the intellect does not simply suffer the course of ideas to occur of itself as it occurs when regulated by mechanical laws, but that it exercises an activity which separates again the ideas that do not belong together; and not merely permits those that belong together to remain so, but is likewise conscious, in the form of general notions or principles, of those valid reasons on account of which they belong together. We have no reason to credit the animals with such a far-reaching reflection, in order to make possible their purposeful behavior and the way they adapt themselves to circumstances. For them the ordinary course of ideas is quite sufficient (since even in it what belongs together is gradually more firmly associated than aught else); just as man also in a great part of his every-day life entrusts himself to it alone.

If therefore the intellect, or thinking, is held to be a distinguishing talent of man, then among the circumstances which favor its cultivation the following may be adduced as pre-eminent: the long helpless childhood, which induces the accumulation of many experiences before it makes conduct possible; the skillfulness of the hand which makes man the born experimenter and permits a multitude of coherent observations; finally, speech — partly because the articulate sounds as symbols for ideas fix their content, and serve to make the combination of many ideas into the object of an inner intuition; partly, and principally, because communication develops further the course of each individual's ideas by means of the stimulating, enriching, and correcting intervention of another's course of thought.

§ **101.** Most definitively is *Reason* regarded as the characteristic of man; and by this is understood the capacity for perceiving eternal verities immediately *per se*, as soon as external experiences have furnished consciousness with the matter of fact, about which these same verities have to express a judgment, — principally one of moral approbation or disapprobation.

We know nothing about a primary psychological origin for these simplest principles of Conscience; and we accordingly have reason to consider them as one of those reactions of the original nature of the spirit, that are never explicable — however often, to be sure, the attempt is made — by the external inducements which they certainly require in order to be awakened. It is, moreover, an indifferent matter whether they are regarded as endowment inborn or as gained by the experience of life; if only it be admitted that, after they have originated within us, they are the expressions of a truth which, although it is discovered by experience, is with respect to its content and its value quite independent thereof.

§ 102. Moral truths exist in order to determine the will. Of this, too, we speak only in the case of men; to the animals we do not impute what they do, because we consider it as the natural result of instinct, but not as the actions of a will.

Instincts are primarily nothing but feelings; and that, chiefly, of pain or at any rate uneasiness. They are wont, however, to be connected with motor impulses, that, in the manner of reflex motions, lead to all kinds of movements by which, after more or less of error, the means are discovered for doing away with the aforesaid pain. It is only after the idea of that action by which the pain is relieved, has combined with feeling, that an instinct, strictly speaking, has been formed, such as has a goal to reach and such that the soul of the animal is instinctively moved by it.

In the same manner do innumerable so-called

'actions' of the human life occur, of which we say, incorrectly,—They are '*willed*.' But the fact simply is, that there has been no will active in order to *prevent* their occurrence.

It is correct to speak of 'willing,' only in case the motives for different actions, and their values, have been compared with full consciousness, and then a decision for one of them has been reached. It is utterly groundless to assert that we even then express by the proposition, "I will," nothing more than the foresight of the future tense, "I shall." This would hold good only in case the verb, whose future tense we employ, has itself the significance of an action in the very conception of which there is inherent an antecedent volition. Otherwise, unprejudiced observation will admit that the peculiar approval of the action conceived, or the adoption of a decision that proceeds from the personal ego,—however impossible it may be to construe such a thing further,—is nevertheless a process in our inner life that is given in fact and is explicable by no mechanism of ideas.

§ **103.** Even if such a nature of the will be recognized, we should still be able to conceive of it as determined in every one of its expressions according to definite laws, in case we rely solely upon *explanatory* science.

Now if Ethics believes that it needs freedom of the will for establishing its views, then Psychology must at least not be misused in the attempt to decide about the possibility of such an assumption, on grounds of so-called experience.

It is not true that we find in our self-observation the determining causes for all our actions. Very frequently we find nothing of the kind. But even where we suppose we find such a thing, the matter is ambiguous. For if the motives for two opposed actions, **a** and **b**, have been for a long time compared in reflection, and then a decision for **a** has taken place, it must always afterward appear as though the reasons for **a** had prevailed over those for **b** by their very strength in a mechanical way; and such an appearance would have to originate in exactly the same manner, if the decision for **a** were in fact accomplished by means of a perfectly undetermined freedom.

To *Metaphysic* must the question be relegated, whether in other regards the conception of such a freedom is capable of being harmonized with our entire way of regarding the world; and to *Practical Philosophy*, the question whether it promises the advantages for the sake of which we venture to make it.

INDEX.

INDEX.

I.

K.

L.

M.

N.

O.

P.

R.

S.

T.

U.

V.

W.